AMERICANS AND CHINESE

AMERICANS AND CHINESE

A HISTORICAL ESSAY AND A BIBLIOGRAPHY

Kwang-Ching Liu

HARVARD UNIVERSITY PRESS

Cambridge, Massachusetts

1963

Library of Congress Catalog Card Number 63–19141
Printed in the United States of America

FOREWORD

In recent decades the serious study of Chinese-American relations has taken on a new urgency. Within the United States these relations have become a major issue at times overshadowing other aspects of our foreign policy as a subject of political controversy. At the other side of the Pacific, the Chinese Communists have begun to reinterpret the historical record in accordance with their own basic doctrines, primarily emphasizing the theme of "imperialism" as the essence of all Western diplomatic, commercial, religious, and cultural activities in China. The need to acquire a thorough and many-sided understanding of the history of our relations with the Chinese has therefore become a practical necessity.

The study of American relations with Japan and Korea has a similar relevance to the contemporary scene. How we "opened" Japan and within a century were involved in war to defeat Japan's militaristic expansion is a story equally as vital, and as tragic, as that of our contacts with China.

American archives in this field are abundant, largely untapped and to some degree unmapped. Very extensive Chinese and Japanese materials are also available in the half-dozen major American Chinese-Japanese libraries, and further materials are being constantly received both from Tokyo and Taipei and from the mainland.

In order to help the growth of this field a committee of the History Department at Harvard University has been sponsoring over the past five years a modest program of fellowships, instruction, bibliographical research, and publication.

Under the auspices of the committee, Herbert Feis, Robert Schwantes, and H. M. Vinacke, as visiting professors, have offered courses of instruction in this field; and a succession of visiting lecturers have spoken to interested students. Several Fellows have been encouraged to pursue the studies necessary to prepare them for teaching and research in this area, and have contributed to instruction at Harvard. A group of young scholars under Dr. K. C. Liu has prepared a series of bibliographical aids that reveal the breadth of the available material, as listed in his preface below.

The present volume is the outgrowth of an extensive survey of archival and published resources in the United States relating to Chinese-American relations, which Dr. Liu has conducted during the past five years. His introductory essay raises many questions and possibilities for research on this whole subject.

Kwang-Ching Liu received his A.B. from Harvard in 1945, his A.M. in 1947, and his Ph.D. in History in 1956. His book *Anglo-American Steamship Rivalry in China, 1862–1874* was published by the Harvard University Press in 1962.

We hope that the opportunities and insights offered in the following pages may stimulate research in a field too long neglected.

Committee on American Far Eastern Policy Studies
Ernest R. May, *Chairman*
John K. Fairbank
Frank Freidel
Oscar Handlin
William L. Langer

Department of History
Harvard University
May 1962

AUTHOR'S PREFACE

AMERICA'S role as a world power has attracted increasing attention from historians, but their concern has been concentrated primarily on the part played by the government. The extensive activities of American individuals and organizations abroad have been touched upon rather lightly, thus far. Moreover, although diplomatic history has received wide coverage, few scholars have studied the effects of American actions upon a particular country — in the economic and cultural as well as political fields.

Yet the activities of individuals and organizations are as much a part of the American record as are those of the government. What is more, in certain large areas of the world such as Asia, contacts with the United States at the nongovernmental level — through traders and entrepreneurs, missionaries, educators, and scientists, and through students and other visitors — had greater effects, on the whole, than any direct activity of the American government. In China America's cultural and economic influence was undoubtedly more important than the impact of her power.

This volume is the result of a preliminary inquiry into American-Chinese relations at the nongovernmental level. It is true that, from 1844 on, American diplomacy was active in supporting the Sino-Western treaty system, and that after the turn of the century the United States took diplomatic action in defense of the Open Door and the territorial integrity of China. At certain junctures — for

example, the period from 1915 to 1922 and during the
Second World War — American power, serving a broad-
ened view of our national interest, plainly contributed
to the cause of China's sovereignty and independence. But
in retrospect, over the whole period since 1784, it may be
said that American long-term cultural and economic influences were more important to China's internal development than the policy of safeguarding the Open Door for
trade and China's territorial integrity. Neither this policy
nor the activities of individuals and organizations sufficed
to prevent the disastrous events in China of recent decades.
But the historian now has the opportunity to inquire into
the record and see where our successes and failures lay.

The present volume is not meant to be a comprehensive
research guide in the proper sense. The field of Chinese-
American relations is as yet too unexplored and unstudied
to permit the evaluation and annotation of all major works,
few though they be. Moreover, it has not seemed feasible
to make a survey of government archives and publications
in greater detail than that provided in the many inventories, finding lists and guides already in existence. My
aim in the following pages has been to raise questions and
suggestions and to indicate unexploited opportunities for
study, new vistas for the historical researcher. The introductory essay, therefore, does not attempt a definitive summary of what has happened in the course of Chinese-
American relations but instead seeks to give some indica-
tion of the nature of American-Chinese contacts and the
areas in which these contacts affected Chinese as well as
American life. As research progresses, many statements
herein will come to need revision. But insofar as it draws
attention to facts and areas of experience previously neg-

lected, this brief survey may help to advance study of the field.

To stimulate research, there are included classified lists of comparatively little-known sources, all in Western languages and mostly of American authorship, which are germane to the study of American-Chinese relations. These are (1) nongovernmental manuscripts and archives in libraries or other depositories in the United States; (2) biographies, memoirs, and published letters of Americans concerned with China and of Chinese who went to the United States; (3) comparatively obscure periodicals and newspapers published by Americans, Chinese, or Europeans in America or in China; and (4) reference works especially useful to the study of the Chinese end of the American-Chinese relationship. These are only a few categories among the vast written records in this field.

Readers of this volume should be familiar with Oscar Handlin, *et al., Harvard Guide to American History* (Cambridge, Mass., 1954), and with Tung-li Yuan, *China in Western Literature: A Continuation of Cordier's "Bibliotheca Sinica"* (New Haven, 1958). Attention is drawn also to the following three bibliographies published at Harvard in 1960: Valentin H. Rabe, *American-Chinese Relations, 1784–1941: Books and Pamphlets Extracted from the Shelf Lists of Widener Library*, 150 pp.; Clayton H. Chu, *American Missionaries in China: Books, Articles and Pamphlets Extracted from the Subject Catalogue of the Missionary Research Library*, 509 pp. in 3 vols.; Robert L. Irick, Ying-shih Yü, and Kwang-Ching Liu, *American-Chinese Relations, 1784–1941: A Survey of Chinese-Language Materials at Harvard*, 296 pp. (all distributed through the Harvard University Press). This last item is an elaborately classified guide to the extensive Chinese sources relevant to this field, which constitute an entire universe awaiting study and correlation with the universe of Western-language sources.

I am grateful to the Committee on American Far Eastern Policy Studies at Harvard for staunch support during the period in which this volume was being prepared. I am deeply indebted to the following individuals who have generously allowed me to draw information from their own researches: Gunther Barth, Dorothy Borg, Jacques M. Downs, Frank H. H. King, Valentin H. Rabe, Edward Rhoads, and James C. Thomson. And I should also like to thank my wife for her invaluable help in the preparation of the manuscript.

K. C. L.

Cambridge, Massachusetts

CONTENTS

I

HISTORICAL PROBLEMS

HISTORICAL PROBLEMS ARISING FROM THE
CONTACTS BETWEEN AMERICANS AND CHINESE

Any historical reassessment of American-Chinese relations must begin by focusing upon the extensive activities of private American individuals and organizations in China. Until America's entry into the Second World War in 1941, the role played by our government in that country was a restricted one. Individuals and organizations — traders and missionaries, scientists and teachers, business firms and mission societies, schools and hospitals, academic and philanthropic foundations — had had far greater influence upon China than any direct activity of the American government. This fact raises the question of the scope and nature of our nongovernmental contact with China, both in its absolute extent and in comparison with that of other peoples.

Judged even by the rough figures thus far available, the extent of the American involvement in China was impressive. In 1870, there were 50 American firms in China; in 1900, 81; and by 1930, the number had increased to 566. In 1870, there were about 200 missionaries in China, representing 12 mission societies; by 1900, the number of missionaries had increased to 1000, representing 28 societies; and by 1930, the total had grown to more than 3000, representing 60 societies. In 1900, there were 6 colleges, 75 secondary schools, and 50 hospitals in China which had been founded under American (mainly mis-

sionary) auspices; by 1930, the number had increased to
14 colleges, 180 schools, and 150 hospitals. These activities
were pluralistic in origin, and not directed by the government. They were nevertheless part of the American
record, analogous in their effects to the economic and cultural programs which the government is today pushing
vigorously in non-Communist Asia.

A second question, arising from this growth of contact,
relates to its over-all influence in the Chinese scene. Here
we are most in need of monographic studies to lay a sound
basis for historical generalizations, which may confirm or
modify the often doctrinaire assumptions, for example, of
foreign missionary promoters at the time or Chinese political propagandists more recently. Privately sponsored
American efforts in China were not always altruistic in
motive. Moreover, they were patently insufficient to help
solve China's manifold problems. In the view of some
Chinese, both then and since, their effects were often even
injurious — and the grievance was the more acutely felt
because for a century American activities in China were
carried on under the Sino-Western "unequal treaties."
Quite possibly the many constructive aspects of this American contact were best known in the United States, and
the undesirable aspects best known in China. The same
activity — say, evangelism — might be esteemed very differ-
ently by observers on the two sides. This field is fraught
with all the problems of cultural relativism and ambiv-
alence.

Similar problems of fact and interpretation arise in the
study of the part played by Chinese as transmitters of
American influence. While over the decades many Americans went to China, many Chinese came to this country
and stayed for some time. A great many laborers and mer-

chants eventually returned to China, as did students who came to gain a Western education. In 1919, there were 955 students from China at American colleges and universities; in 1930, there were 1306. Like the traders and missionaries who went out to China, the "America-returned Chinese" were carriers of American influence. There arise the questions: how great was this influence? how was it exercised? and how was it modified in the course of being transmitted?

TRADERS AND ENTREPRENEURS

Of the various aspects of American-Chinese relations, commerce was originally the most important. It was mainly for the sake of the tea trade that, in the late eighteenth century — as soon as the Revolution made it possible — Americans sailed halfway round the globe to Canton. For more than one hundred and fifty years, the trade between America and China expanded steadily. In the middle of the nineteenth century, the United States imported annually more than $13,500,000 worth of merchandise from China and exported more than $8,900,000 worth to that country. Seventy years later, in 1920, these figures were, respectively, $211,000,000 and $169,000,000.

Economic historians have yet to appraise the exact proportion of our total trade which the China trade represented, at various times during its history, and the precise role which it played in the development of America. But enough is known to pose many fascinating questions. Presumably, the China trade was more important to the United States before the middle of the nineteenth century than afterward. It was not just that the Canton market provided the primary incentive for ventures on the West Coast and among the islands of the Pacific — and thus laid the foundation for later American acquisition of some of these territories. The accumulation of wealth and business experience that resulted from the China trade was of great value in the development of the East and the Middle West. As early as the 1830's, some China traders in New England and New York had turned investors in productive enterprises at home. And the China trade furnished not only the crucial initial capital, but also the key entrepreneurial personnel for the early Midwestern railroads — especially the Michigan Central and the Chicago, Burlington, and Quincy systems. The financial and business methods employed by a Perkins, a Sturgis, or a Forbes in ventures in the distant China seas proved most valuable in enterprises in Iowa or Illinois.

The China trade was never again such a stimulus to the American economy. But in the last decade of the nineteenth century, when American manufacturers worried about a saturated domestic market, they came to regard the supposed buying power of China's millions as their great opportunity for the future. In 1899, China actually absorbed close to 50 percent of America's cotton textile exports (manufactured chiefly by mills in Massachusetts and in the South). By the first decade of the new century, China had become Standard Oil's largest foreign market outside of Europe — consuming more than 2,000,000 barrels of kerosene annually, in good years. By the second decade, China emerged as the leading foreign market for American cigarettes, helping to raise the price of tobacco and of tobacco fields in the Carolinas and in Virginia. The total share of China in America's foreign trade was never more than 3 or 4 percent. Nonetheless this trade was important to certain sections and certain groups.

Problems related to the effects of American trade upon

China are much more entangled in political passions and are correspondingly in need of dispassionate research. Before 1860 the Americans played a part in bringing upon China at least two evils — the traffic in opium and in coolie laborers. As early as 1805, American merchants, in their efforts to find a commodity that would sell in Canton, had begun to ship small quantities of Turkish or Persian opium to China. After 1830, when the drug trade between British India and China grew very rapidly, many American vessels carried Patna or Malwa from Calcutta or Bombay to China, on behalf of British or Parsee constituents. Some of the finest Boston-built clipper ships of the 1840's and 1850's were employed in delivering drugs on the Chinese beaches, in defiance of the "mandarin boats." Opium shipped by Americans was perhaps never more than one-tenth of the total quantity imported into China, and after 1860, very few American firms continued in the trade. But American firms were involved in this traffic for as long as half a century, and its effects were fully as injurious as many Americans of the period — including missionaries in China and publicists at home — repeatedly said.

Even more iniquitous than the opium trade was the coolie trade — the traffic in able-bodied Chinese, abducted or otherwise procured from Macao, Canton, or Amoy, destined for hard labor and frequently for early death in Latin America — for example, in Peru and Cuba. As far as is known, American mercantile firms in China had nothing to do with this trade. There is no evidence that any citizen of the United States was ever connected with the notorious baracoons of Macao and Amoy, operated chiefly by Macao Portuguese and Latin Americans. But the high profits from carrying coolies across the Pacific did, in the 1850's, attract many American owners of tramp sailing vessels, particularly those accustomed to navigation in the Caribbean or South American waters. In 1857, at least 31 American ships accepted charters to carry coolies from South China. The unspeakable conditions on board the coolie ships — as evidenced by the case of the *Waverley* in September 1855, when 260 Chinese died of suffocation in the course of the passage to South America — have their place in American maritime history. Even after 1862, when Congress passed a bill applying slave-trade legislation to the traffic in Chinese coolies, certain American ships still engaged in it, using the protection of foreign colors.

The opium trade and the transportation of Chinese coolies are permanent blots in the record of the America-China trade and writers in mainland China have not been slow in recent years to point this out, sometimes with a tendency to exaggeration which is understandable even if their facts are not substantiated. It is the duty of historians to examine the record and set it forth in detail and in due proportion. Thorough study may support the conclusion that both these evils were incidental to the main course of the trade. Meanwhile American trade and investment, though only one of the many factors in the modern Chinese economy, may be given their due as contributing to China's development.

Beginning in the late eighteenth century, the major undertaking of the American traders was to bring tea and silk from China to this country — and to Europe as well, whenever conditions permitted. In the late 1830's, the amount of tea imported annually into the United States from China exceeded 16,500,000 pounds. By the 1890's, it had increased to more than 45,000,000 pounds. By the latter period, the United States also imported more than 1,450,000 pounds of Chinese raw silk. Over the decades the American trade presumably contributed to the prosperity of the tea- and silk-producing districts. It is also likely that toward the end of the nineteenth century the American traders injured Chinese rural handicrafts, when they imported into China large quantities of cotton piece goods which competed with Chinese fabrics. In the forty-five years between 1850 and 1895, the total annual value of American cotton cloth shipped into China increased from $1,200,000 to $3,000,000; by the late 1890's the figure had climbed to $7,000,000. The trade seems in any case to have been profitable to Chinese traders. Many Chinese merchants who sold tea and silk to Western firms — such as Russell & Co.'s compradors, Choping and Koofunsing — were among the leading capitalists of Shanghai. Similarly in the areas where the sales of American drills and sheetings were concentrated, in North China and Manchuria, the Chinese piece-goods merchants were usually the most affluent in their communities. Plainly, the balance between these various tendencies cannot be drawn out of hand.

In the nineteenth-century treaty ports, the American firms often branched out into enterprises involving long-term local investment. In 1862, Russell & Co. founded a joint-stock steamship company in Shanghai for the carrying trade on the Yangtze River and on the China coast. Of the company's initial capital of Tls. 1,000,000 ($1,358,000), one-third was subscribed by the Americans themselves, another third by the British merchants in China, and the remainder by Chinese comprador-merchants. Through the process of plowing back earnings, the company's capital was increased to Tls. 3,000,000 in the early 1870's, this sum being invested in eighteen steamships and other properties. Russell & Co. also founded, in 1878, the first successful machine-operated silk filature in Shanghai. Other American firms, Wetmore & Co. and the American Trading Company, pioneered in modern cotton textile manufacturing. The former attempted to establish a mill as early as 1881 but failed to obtain the Chinese government's approval; the latter succeeded, after the Treaty of Shimonoseki in 1895, in establishing a plant of 40,000 rings. As was the case with Russell & Co.'s shipping company — which competed with and in 1877 was sold to a Chinese government-sponsored steamship company — American ventures in the cotton textile industry stimulated rival Chinese efforts.

In the twentieth century, the American China trade grew apace. Between 1900 and 1920, the total value of imports from China increased from $28,000,000 to $211,-000,000, and exports to China, from $24,000,000 to $169,-800,000. Among the imports from China the new staples (in the order of their importance as of 1920) were raw silk, hides and skins, vegetable and wood oil, furs, bristles, eggs. This trade was undoubtedly a stimulus to the rural economy in many parts of China. Among American exports to China, the major items as of 1920 were iron and steel manufactures, petroleum products (mainly kerosene), industrial machinery, cigarettes, raw tobacco, chemicals. Thanks to careful organization and persevering sales campaigns, American cigarettes and kerosene were widely marketed in China. It may be arguable that the contribution to Chinese life made by the kerosene lamp compensated for the injury done the producers of vegetable oil, tallow dips, and candles. One may also try, at his peril, to evaluate whether cigarette-smoking benefited the Chinese and their economy.

As China's industrialization got under way machinery and other iron and steel products from the United States played an important role. In 1901, the total value of industrial machinery exported from the United States to China was only $284,000 and other iron and steel manufactures amounted to only $554,000. By 1920, these exports had increased to $18,200,000 and $24,980,000. (For comparison, it may be noted that in 1920, the total value of petroleum products exported from the United States to China was $19,470,000; cigarettes, $16,080,000; and raw tobacco, $13,300,000.) In 1923, the United States provided 58.7 percent of China's total imports of rails; 80.8 percent of copper wire; 48.4 percent of screws. It was estimated that, in 1924, almost all the machinery in China's modern flour mills, at least 25.8 percent of China's machine-driven spindles, and 15.3 percent of her power looms were American made.

Besides selling machines and industrial materials to the Chinese, the Americans continued to invest in modern transport and industry in China. The significance of this activity for the American economy — the economic underpinning of American interest in China — is still a moot point.

Similar uncertainty adheres to the actual American financial impact on China in the era of dollar diplomacy. The grandiose plans for loans to the Chinese government entertained by the nation's financiers were well publicized. In the twenty-five years after 1895, there were many occasions when such loans, especially those for the purpose of railway construction, were considered by investment firms like Kuhn, Loeb & Co. and J. P. Morgan & Co., and such banks as the Chase National and the First National of New York. These plans had the support of the American government. However, although the Americans at different times held concessions to build as many as seven Chinese railways, they never actually built them. During the early warlord period, between 1915 and 1921, seven loans were made by American banks (or other firms) to the Peking government, amounting to a total of $25,555,000. These proved to be unprofitable for, aside from three loans totaling $12,500,000, neither principal nor interest was paid the lenders by the warlord regimes. And it is certain that, except for an advance of $6,500,000, used for building wireless stations, the Chinese government did not employ the funds for any constructive end.

Nevertheless, in less spectacular ways, there was a continuous flow of American capital into China. Much of it was to meet the needs of the growing trade. As of 1930, the total American investment in China in connection with trading business has been estimated at $73,000,000. This included installations, merchandise stocked, and capital in auxiliary enterprises, such as banks and insurance companies. In addition there were small, but by no means unimportant, American investments in transport and industrial enterprises: $6,200,000 in shipping (mainly small steamers that plied the Upper Yangtze); $20,500,000 in manufacturing (mainly in carpets, electrical equipment, wood products, and egg products). The last figure does not include American interests in the British-American Tobacco Company, a London firm founded in 1902 by James B. Duke of Durham, North Carolina, and his British partners, Duke serving as president until 1922. In the decade before the First World War, the B.A.T. and its subsidiaries established cigarette factories (with the capacity to produce eight or ten million cigarettes per day) in five Chinese cities; and the B.A.T.'s campaign to introduce American tobacco seed to Chinese farmers resulted in the wide cultivation of this cash crop in Shantung and four other provinces. Meanwhile, a Chinese tobacco industry was springing up. The Nanyang Brothers, the B.A.T.'s chief Chinese rival, was established in 1905; by 1927, there were some 180 Chinese cigarette factories. Here again, the American influence remains to be evaluated.

In 1929, the American and Foreign Power Company invested $40,000,000 in the largest power plant in Shanghai, with a capacity of 183,500 kilowatts. The cheap electricity made available by this plant greatly benefited the numerous industrial plants in the Shanghai area. Although their effects were restricted to a narrow sector of the Chinese economy, such investments undoubtedly contributed to the modernization process.

MISSIONARIES

American-Chinese relations on the cultural-intellectual plane present even more complex problems than on the economic. Nothing in modern history is in greater need of analysis than the missionary movement, in both its causes and its effects (two very different types of phenomena!). While traders and entrepreneurs were concerned with China primarily for profit, American missionaries were interested in the propagation of the Christian faith and auxiliary services in education, medicine, and philanthropy. Beginning in 1829, when the American Board of Commissioners for Foreign Missions sent two missionaries to Canton, American missionary work in China expanded steadily for more than a century. By 1930, there were more than 3000 American missionaries in China, while the total annual remittance from the United States to the missions there exceeded $7,700,000. In terms of the personnel involved and of financial investment (which included the dimes and quarters collected on many a Sunday all over the United States), the missionary enterprise represented a large as well as a longstanding effort.*

The missionary movement needs to be studied as the outgrowth of developments within the American scene. For the course of events in American religious life was such as to prompt thousands of young men and women to dedicated service abroad. The movement reveals a deeply purposeful America — obeying the frequently quoted biblical injunction, "Go ye into all the world, and preach the gospel to every creature," and adopting the famous watchword of the Student Volunteer Movement (founded in 1886), "The evangelization of the world in this generation." The work of the missionaries, moreover, reflected certain specific trends in church life at home — the zeal for education that resulted in the founding of numerous denominational colleges; medical and other community services being viewed as a religious concern; and the championing of social justice.

How were these concerns expressed in a country such as China, with its peculiar problems? While the home back-

---

* Although European Catholics had long been very active in China, American Catholic missions in that country began very late. It was not until 1918 that the Catholic Foreign Mission Society of America (Maryknoll mission, founded in 1911) sent four missionaries to China. By 1926 it had developed work in three areas — Kwangtung, Kwangsi, and the southeastern part of Manchuria. The American Jesuits commenced their work in China in 1928, concentrating in Kiangsu province. Since I am here concerned with a general view of the American missionary effort from 1830 to the 1930's, the following discussion is based chiefly on the Protestant record.

ground of the missionary movement — sentiments, ideas, and the practical problems of recruitment and support — should be systematically studied, the effects of the missionaries' work abroad must be viewed in the completely different context of an alien and perhaps, in some ways, more sophisticated culture.

Students who have taken a fresh look at the missionary record in China are impressed by Chinese hostility toward Christianity. Particularly in the nineteenth century, there was a widespread movement among the Chinese literati against the missionaries, who spread "heterodox" ideas and wished to settle in their midst. Among the more than two hundred "antimissionary cases" brought before the Chinese government in the forty years *before* the Boxer rising of 1900, at least forty involved American missionaries. A basic cause of hostility was, undoubtedly, the gentry-officials' abhorrence of heterodoxy. They were offended not so much by the missionary's mysterious rites and medical practices as by his attacks on cherished Chinese institutions. The American Board mission, for example, distributed in the 1870's a Chinese-language tract entitled *Pien hsiao lun* (On filial piety), assailing ancestor worship. Moreover, the gentry-officials were resentful of the missionary's extraterritorial status (as provided for in the Sino-Western treaties) and his desire to rent or purchase properties in Chinese provincial towns for chapels, dispensaries, or living quarters. Dispute over missionary residence often provided the immediate cause for antimissionary riots.

While the missionaries' efforts often led to conflict, did they also contribute to Chinese life? This is a question with many ramifications. As far as evangelism itself was concerned, the results were limited. The total number of

Protestant communicants in China (including those of European as well as American missions) was only 37,000 in 1889 and 178,000 in 1905; few would claim that, then or later, any spectacular spiritual movement arose among the Chinese Christians. The influence of the missionaries must be sought outside the small circle of converts and indeed outside proselytism itself.

If only indirectly, Christian proselytism did bring to China values not traditionally emphasized in her culture. The Pauline spiritual experience so fervently invoked by the Protestant evangelist was evidently more intense and thoroughgoing than any offered by contemporary Buddhism or Taoism and involved a profound revolution in conduct. While the missionaries, predictably, inveighed against sinfulness and idol worship, they also assailed those aspects of Chinese custom and conventional morality which violated Christian charity and ideas of personal worth — infanticide, female slavery, and concubinage. Missionary writings on the humanitarian shortcomings of Chinese society inspired such books as *Sheng-shih wei-yen* (Warnings to a prosperous age), by the Cantonese ex-comprador, Cheng Kuan-ying. By the 1890's, Christianity had patently had an impact on the world of the Chinese scholar. It was Christian proselytism that inspired K'ang Yu-wei's views on China's need for a Confucian *chiao* (religion). And one detects elements of Christian ethics in T'an Ssu-t'ung's concepts of *p'ing-teng* (equality) and *jen* (benevolence or love).

Although the majority of the missionaries were primarily concerned with evangelism, others labored to bring science and other modern knowledge to the Chinese. Through the nineteenth century, the unpretentious magazines and books published by the missionaries were often the best source of Western learning in China. *Tung-Hsi-yang k'ao mei-yueh t'ung-chi chuan* (Chinese Monthly Magazine), first published in 1833 at Canton and edited by the American Board missionary Elijah Bridgman and others, contained articles on the steam engine, world geography, the British and American systems of government, and the life of George Washington. And in *Wan-kuo kung-pao* (The Globe Magazine or the Review of the World), first published in 1875 and edited by the Southern Methodist Young J. Allen and others, there are articles on physics and mathematics, on nineteenth-century European history, on education and welfare as China's primary needs and administrative reform as the prerequisite for national strength. After the Sino-Japanese War of 1894–1895, the circulation of this magazine increased to more than 30,000 copies, and pirated editions were sold in several Chinese provinces. It undoubtedly contributed to the reform movement of the late 1890's.

As Western learning made greater progress in the Chinese publishing world, especially through translations made by Chinese who had studied in Japan or the West, missionary magazines soon lost their importance. But missionary-sponsored schools and colleges continued to have an important place as the institutions where subjects such as natural sciences and mathematics were taught efficiently. Mission schools of academy grade began to teach modern subjects seriously in the 1870's, and before 1905 there were already 6 institutions of collegiate rank — all sponsored by American missions. Twenty years later, in 1925, the 333 Protestant "middle schools" had a total enrollment of 25,597 students, and the 16 colleges had 2,811 students. In natural sciences, mathematics, and other Western subjects, the standards set by Christian middle schools were unsurpassed in modern China — as many eminent Chinese scientists, who owe their early training to mission schools, can testify. The Christian colleges, too, maintained comparatively high standards, and in the 1920's were often the outstanding institutions of higher education in their provinces. Even in the 1930's, such universities as Yenching, Nanking, and Lingnan could hold their own against the best Chinese national universities.

The missionary educational effort had certain incidental social effects. Missionary schools for women were established in the 1860's, and colleges in the 1900's. As late as 1910 these were still the only places in China where women had the same educational opportunity as men. By discrediting arranged marriage and by offering women professional training, Christian schools and colleges made a signal contribution to the liberation of the Chinese woman. These schools and colleges helped also in providing opportunities for education to underprivileged families — typically through the free tuition or modest scholarships allowed to sons and daughters of Chinese Christians. Although among the graduates of Christian schools and colleges many were attracted by lucrative posts in government or business, there were also many who pursued a teaching career. At least in the case of such institutions as Shantung Christian University or Hwa Nan College (Foochow), a large percentage of the alumni did return to work in their homes in inland towns, particularly in connection with church service.

The missionaries also set high standards in their medical services. As early as 1876, there were 16 hospitals and 24 dispensaries in China operated under Protestant auspices. By 1925, there were 301 such hospitals and 496 dispensaries — more than half the hospitals being operated by

American missions. In the memoirs of nineteenth-century doctors one often reads of how even the antiforeign gentry and officials would change their attitude after accepting the help of the Western physician. But the benefits of such work were extended to all classes of Chinese. Many a Christian doctor serving a Chinese town exemplified a combination of technical competence and humanitarian concern which deeply impressed those about him.

The missionaries, with the help of lay organizations in the United States, advanced medical education and public health work in China. By 1925, there were four major medical schools in that country under mission auspices. One of them, the Hsiang Ya in Changsha (reorganized in 1913), was unique in that it was sponsored jointly by the missionaries (the Yale Missionary Society) and the local Chinese government. Another, the Peking Union Medical College (founded in 1919), had the advantage of wholehearted support from the Rockefeller Foundation — some $33,000,000 for the fourteen years between 1919 and 1933. By this latter date, the P.U.M.C. had won renown as the best medical school and the best hospital in all Asia. The Chinese doctors and technicians trained at P.U.M.C. and at other Christian medical schools provided the core of China's modern medical personnel, in government as well as private service.

Although the majority of American educational and medical missionaries restricted their activities to China's cities and towns, large and small, others belatedly concentrated on the peasants — who, after all, composed some 80 percent of the population. In 1914 a College of Agriculture and Forestry was founded at the University of Nanking. Under the leadership of John H. Reisner and J. Lossing Buck, and in cooperation with Cornell University, studies were undertaken of the technical needs of Chinese agriculture — seeds and fertilizers, the prevention of plant and animal diseases. Beginning with only 29 students, in 1930 the college had an enrollment of 163. In that year its activities included the organization of irrigation and storage projects and of farmers' cooperatives at several experimental stations; the dissemination of new information and of improved seed varieties through extension meetings all over China; and the preparation of an economic and social survey resulting in J. Lossing Buck's *Chinese Farm Economy* (1930) and *Land Utilization in China* (1937). In 1930, two other Christian universities in China had developed faculties in agriculture or animal husbandry; and by the mid-1930's, several missions had established "agricultural middle schools" — for example, in Foochow and in Paoting, Hopeh.

While the agricultural missionaries concentrated on technical questions, others began to search for practical programs of rural service. In language reminiscent of the "social gospel" at home, the National Christian Council (the coordinating body of the churches in China) had passed a resolution in 1922 expressing deep concern over rural poverty and had appointed a committee to study rural problems. The missionaries also drew ideas and support from lay sources. Beginning in the early 1920's, they participated in the work of the China International Famine Relief Commission, which built roads, canals, and embankments, dug wells, and provided funds for farmers' credit cooperatives in several provinces north of the Yangtze. In the late 1920's, rural-minded missionaries in North China helped to experiment with the new techniques of mass education developed by James Y. C. Yen, a Yale-educated former Y.M.C.A. secretary, who had been disappointed by the church's role in this field. By 1929, three years after Mr. Yen founded the Tinghsien experiment in mass education, missionaries in different parts of China also had initiated rural service programs in selected regions. In Shunhuacheng, thirteen miles outside Nanking, the Rural Church Department of the Nanking Theological Seminary conducted a program that emphasized agricultural extension and mutual help as well as proselytizing. In the farm communities outside Paoting, Hugh Hubbard of the American Board had begun the combined program of literacy classes, health reform, and. agricultural improvement that he so successfully conducted at Fanchiachuang (near Paoting) after 1933.

The needs of the Chinese peasant also drew the attention of nonmissionary philanthropic organizations in the United States. As early as 1911, the American Red Cross gave $400,000 for famine relief in China, and up through the 1920's, it stood ready to help in the long-delayed Hwai River conservation program (which Yuan Shih-k'ai and the early warlord governments had hoped to undertake.) During the great North China famine of 1920–1921, secular as well as church groups contributed to the American Committee for the China Famine Fund. The proceeds were later expended by the China International Famine Relief Commission, whose staff included many lay experts as well as missionaries. By 1936, the commission had spent a total of $50,000,000; it had dug 5000 wells, built 2000 miles of roads, 300 miles of drainage canals, and 1000 miles of river embankments, and assisted farmers' credit cooperatives with a total membership of 200,000. Beginning in the late 1920's, several organizations in the

United States, including the Milbank Memorial Fund, had contributed to James Yen's mass education project at Tinghsien — which proved effective not only in eliminating illiteracy, but also in helping the farmers to organize themselves for agricultural improvement programs and community services. In 1934, acting upon the proposal of its vice president, Selskar M. Gunn, the Rockefeller Foundation embarked on a $300,000-per-year program to train personnel for rural service and to encourage the application of the social sciences to rural problems. The training programs at Tinghsien and at another center planned by Yen in South China received the largest of the new grants. At Tsining, Shantung, another center was established which emphasized problems of "civil and social administration." When the Japanese invasion interrupted the program in 1937, there were 160 college students in training at Tsining, and by arrangement with the Chinese government a professor from Yenching University was serving as the *hsien* magistrate.

This brief review, drawn from a few preliminary researches, indicates the great variety and pioneering character of American missionary activities in China. Detailed studies of these enterprises, for which extensive records exist, are urgently needed both to provide an inside story of the Christian approach to China and also to lay a basis for appraising its part in the modernization of China as a whole. Rightly or wrongly, much of this missionary activity is now stigmatized on the Chinese mainland as "cultural imperialism." Obviously, more must be known of the record before it can be evaluated either pro or con, and the activities of representatives of one culture working in another must be looked at from more than one point of view.

Similar problems of cultural contact and conflict appear at the American end of our relations with China. While many Americans crossed the Pacific to gain profit, to spread the gospel, or to render service, the movement of people was not onesided, and from the middle of the nineteenth century on, many Chinese visited the United States. By 1873, a quarter century after the beginning of the Gold Rush to the Sacramento Valley, there were 62,500 Chinese in California and some 20,000 in other states and territories. The year before, there had arrived in this country a group of 30 Chinese students, the first of the more than 20,000 who came to the United States for education between 1872 and 1948, many of them destined, in their later lives, to play an important part in China's development.

The early experience of Chinese laborers in this country is a most tragic chapter in the history of American-Chinese relations. The Chinese made a great contribution to the development of the American West. They cleared and drained tule lands and worked in inferior placers abandoned by other miners. They built roads and gradings and provided the chief part of the labor force that made possible the completion of the Transcontinental Railroad in 1869 and of the Southern Pacific system in the ensuing decades. Yet the Chinese were on the whole the most unfairly treated group of newcomers. Beginning in the 1850's, in a California where the rule of law was still rudimentary, they were subject to discriminatory tax laws; they were not permitted to testify in court and were excluded from the rights of citizenship. In mining camps and in settlements, they were assaulted, robbed, and murdered, with only a few of these cases ever brought to justice. In the 1870's, when the rise of militant labor unions coincided with economic upheaval in California, the Chinese suffered ever more flagrant abuses. In the San Francisco area, in 1877–1878, lawless elements committed arson, robbery, and murder against the Chinese; in Truckee, in November 1878, the entire Chinese population of about a thousand was driven out of town. Until the early 1890's, frequent anti-Chinese riots occurred in other states and territories. In Rock Springs, Wyoming, in 1885, twenty-eight Chinese were killed in one day. At Snake River in Oregon, in 1887, ten Chinese gold miners were robbed and murdered by men masquerading as cowboys. The incidents reflect the strains in an unstable frontier society; they are among the darkest stains on the history of liberty in the United States.

The Chinese were the first ethnic group to be barred from the United States by law. As early as 1868, the Democrats in California had demanded that Chinese immigration be stopped. During the 1870's, anti-Chinese passion having been further inflamed by hard times and by Kearneyism, even the Republicans demanded strongly that "the Chinese must go!" Owing partly to the pressure of trade unions in the East (which shared with those in California the fear of Chinese competitors and strikebreakers), but chiefly on account of the decisive importance of Californian votes in national politics, Congress bowed to Western sentiment and in 1879 passed a bill restricting the entry of Chinese laborers for ten years. This bill was vetoed by President Hayes on the ground that it contravened the Burlingame Treaty of 1868. However, after the treaty provisions were modified in an agreement between China and the United States in 1880, a new Chinese Exclusion Act became law in 1882. Thereafter, before almost every presidential election, a new act was passed by Congress to meet California's demand for more rigid exclusion: the Scott Act of 1888, which limited the return to the United States of those Chinese who had visited China temporarily; the Geary Law of 1892, which renewed restriction for ten years and required the registration of all Chinese in the United States; and a new bill in 1902, which excluded Chinese laborers permanently.

Such legislation, together with the anti-Chinese riots, provoked deep Chinese resentment. The Chinese Consolidated Benevolent Association (the so-called Six Companies) repeatedly protested to the California state government, to Congress, and to the President. There is evidence that the reports of the United States government's initial refusal to pay indemnity for the victims of the Rock Springs massacre, publicized in the Chinese newspapers at the treaty ports, contributed to an antimissionary riot in a Yangtze port in 1886. Meanwhile, the unnecessarily harsh manner in which immigration officials administered the Chinese exclusion acts drew many complaints. Although the laws applied only to Chinese laborers, many merchants and students suffered humiliation and hardship at the port of entry. In 1903, the whole Chinese colony in Boston, consisting of several thousand people, was surrounded by police and 234 arrested, so that 40 deportable persons might be located. In 1904, the Chinese merchants invited to attend the Louisiana exposition had to travel under the surveillance of the immigration agents, who wished to make sure that they returned to their ships.

Incidents of this nature, together with the accumulated grievances of the Chinese in the United States, prompted an anti-American boycott in 1905, specifically in protest against the pending treaty negotiations regarding immigration arrangements. The boycott was organized by merchants in Shanghai, Canton, and five other coastal cities and supported by students at China's modern schools (missionary institutions included). It lasted in some cities for six months, caused heavy losses to American merchants, and played a significant role in the growth of nationalism in China.

Despite their mortifying experiences, the Chinese in the United States found new opportunities. Due to the fact that many elected to return to China, and because there were comparatively few women among the immigrants, the total Chinese population in this country declined from 107,500 in 1890 to 61,600 in 1920. However, among those who stayed, including second-generation Chinese, many found new homes in other parts of the nation, and new kinds of employment. In 1890, of the 107,500 Chinese in the United States, 85,000 were in the Pacific states and 11,500 in the Rocky Mountain states, only 4,690 being in the Middle Atlantic states and 2,300 in the Middle West; by 1920, of the total of 61,600, there were still 34,200 in the Pacific and 4,340 in the Mountain states, but the number in the Middle Atlantic states had increased to 8,800 and in the Middle West to 6,700. While in 1890, only 30.3 percent of the Chinese population was in cities of 100,000 and over, by 1920 56.2 percent resided in such urban centers. The erstwhile miners, railroad workers, and factory hands had now moved into modest but independent occupations which invited no rancor from organized labor. In 1920, among the 45,600 gainfully employed Chinese in the United States, there were 982 laundry owners and 11,577 laundry workers; 1,685 owners of restaurants and noodle parlors and 2,810 waiters or waitresses; 7,477 connected with commercial firms of all sizes and descriptions (including 4,313 owners of retail stores and 1,658 salesmen or saleswomen); 4,256 connected with manufacturing (including 1,968 associated with food industries and 942 with construction work) ; 790 in transport enterprises (presumably including the staff of the China Mail S.S. Co. of San Francisco, founded in 1915). In addition, there were 794 Chinese in clerical employment and 186 pursuing professional careers, including American government service. By the 1920's there were Chinatowns in twenty-eight American cities, providing centers for social life as well as for the restaurant and curio businesses.

While the economic situation of the Chinese improved, their opportunity to gain citizenship increased. Until 1943, the first-generation Chinese were barred from naturalization by law; but their children born here were of course Americans. In 1900, there were 9,000 native-born among a total Chinese population of 89,800; in 1920, 18,500 among 61,600. For decades after 1885, in San Francisco and in a few other Western cities, the Oriental children, many of whom had not learned English at home, went to elementary schools especially established for them. But, even in San Francisco, there was no segregation of Chinese pupils in junior or senior high schools. In the nation as a whole, the school attendance among Chinese was high. Statistics for 1930 show that the percentage of Chinese children attending school was generally higher than that of white children of native parentage — by 4.9 percent for the ages from fourteen to fifteen; 19.7 percent for the ages from sixteen to seventeen; 20 percent for the ages from eighteen to twenty. Only in the youngest age group of seven to thirteen was the Chinese percentage (96.0) one decimal behind. The number of American-born Chinese attending college steadily increased; in 1941 there were 863. The Chinese-Americans were finding many opportunities opening up for them, in science, engineering, medicine, architecture, business, aviation, and the arts, to mention a few of their favorite pursuits.

This mixed record of Chinese hardship and success, native American animosity and acceptance, invites comparison with the experience of other minority groups in the United States. It can contribute also to study of the acculturation of immigrant communities, in addition to its specific importance as a chapter in the story of Chinese-American relations.

Finally, there is an opportunity to trace the influence exerted in modern China by one of the most vigorous and yet little studied of the many communities of Chinese overseas, namely, that in the United States.

Over the years, how much did the Chinese community in the United States contribute to China economically? Until the 1920's, the majority of the first-generation Chinese eventually returned to China. (This was due to family ties and their idea of the good life; they had always intended to return, to enjoy their declining years.) An estimate based on inquiry at the banks in Hongkong and in the United States in 1928–1930 showed that as much as $42,000,000 was remitted to China annually by the Chinese in the United States. Much of this money went into consumption and into real estate — the new shops and houses in the towns and villages in the emigrant districts in the Pearl River Valley, properties in such cities as Toyshan and Canton. It was the capital of America-returned Chinese that built the railway between Toyshan and Sinhwui. Overseas Chinese capital was a key factor in helping the Canton area recover from the ill effects of revolution and warlordism in the period from 1911 to 1927.

The American Chinese contributed to political causes in China. At the turn of the century, the Gee Kung Tong (or Chinese Freemasons, a collective name for several offshoots of the Triad Society in America) had supported K'ang Yu-wei's movement for a constitutional monarchy under Emperor Kuang Hsü. In 1903, Sun Yat-sen (who had spent his youth in the Chinese community in Hawaii, where his brother was a merchant) was sworn in as a "Freemason," and thereafter he sought the support of this tong, as well as that of young second-generation Chinese, who in 1909 organized the branches of Sun's revolutionary party, the T'ung Meng Hui, in San Francisco and New York. In 1911, when Sun came to the United States for the third time in eight years, he arranged for the American members of the T'ung Meng Hui to join the Freemasons' Association, and he also received the largest donation he had had from the United States up to that time, $20,000 — which proved a timely help in a partisan rising in South China. After the success of the revolution, at least 24 American Chinese went to China and offered their services to the new government, and in the campaign against Yuan Shih-k'ai's monarchical scheme in 1916, the Chinese in the United States again gave money — this time more than half a million dollars — and sent forth two groups to participate in the campaign. Chinese-American enthusiasm for revolution in China declined thereafter, although the community continued to make financial contributions to various causes such as famine and war relief, the nascent Kuomintang air force in the 1930's, and the war against Japan. Most of this interesting story remains as yet unexplored.

In the period that saw the gradual assimilation of the second-generation Chinese by the American culture, another group of Chinese in this country increased in number — the students who came from China for education or training, mostly in colleges and universities. Before 1901, only 57 students of Chinese citizenship had entered American colleges and universities; the figure rose sharply thereafter. In the twenty years between 1901 and 1920, 2406 students entered such institutions, and from 1921 to 1940, 5474 Chinese enrolled. Although the total was comparatively small, this group was obviously of great importance to China's development. Only a few of their personal histories are as yet available.

Chinese students in the United States were more privileged than the Chinatown Chinese. The Chinese laborers who came to this country in the nineteenth century were almost all of peasant background; but the students from China in the twentieth century were mostly drawn from the upper classes — children of officials, gentry, and city-dwelling business and professional men. A large percentage were recipients of scholarships and other aid. Even in the nineteenth century, Chinese students came to the United States with the help of missionaries, for example, Yung Wing (Yale, 1854), and Hü King-eng (Women's Medical College, Philadelphia, 1894). In 1872–1874, the Ch'ing government sent 120 boys to participate in its educational mission at Hartford, Connecticut, headed by

Yung Wing; this project, unfortunately, was discontinued in 1881. With the Manchu reform in the 1900's, Chinese officials again planned to send students to America. And, after 1909, when the United States returned $12,000,000 of China's Boxer indemnity payments — to be followed by further remission after 1924 — a regular system was established for organizing and financing the education of Chinese in America. Between 1909 and 1929, more than 1100 students came to this country under the auspices of Tsing Hua College (established in 1911 for the purpose of preparing students for American colleges and universities.) In addition, several hundred scholars without such preparation were given fellowships on the basis of competitive examination, after 1929 as well as before. This system was designed to encourage talent; and not a few of those selected came from comparatively poor families. But they had at least had an early education that qualified them for Tsing Hua, or for the competitive examination.

Whatever their social origins, their fields of specialization indicate the students' aspirations or their views of China's needs. Statistics show that the largest number of students from China elected engineering, business, and economics (the latter being considered almost as technical training), and education. A substantial number chose pure science and mathematics; political science, sociology, and law; agriculture and medicine; and even literature and history. The following figures are for all students of Chinese citizenship (and therefore do not include the second-generation Chinese) enrolled in American colleges and universities to 1953. They indicate the twenty most attractive fields of concentration out of a total of fifty-seven fields which Chinese students in the United States are known to have taken up.

Field of concentration	*Number of students*
Business administration (or commerce)	1562
Economics	1122
Education	943
Chemistry	854
General engineering	804
Civil engineering	777
General arts	747
Mechanical engineering	681
Political science	615
Electrical engineering	544
Sociology	445
Agriculture	408
Medicine	373
English studies	284
History	269
Law	266
Religion	265
Physics	255
General science	252
Mathematics	251

The Chinese had the opportunity to pursue these studies at major centers of learning in the United States. A total of 370 American colleges and universities conferred degrees on students from China. But over the years, it was such institutions as Columbia, Michigan, the Massachusetts Institute of Technology, Harvard, and Illinois that attracted the largest number. The twenty that did the most up to 1953 to help train students from China were as follows:

Institution	Number of degrees conferred
Columbia University	1834
University of Michigan	1300
Massachusetts Institute of Technology	734
Harvard University	647
University of Illinois	603
New York University	596
University of Pennsylvania	511
University of Chicago	463
University of Wisconsin	410
Cornell University	387
University of Minnesota	366
University of Washington (Seattle)	306
Ohio State University	283
Yale University	273
University of California	269
Stanford University	265
University of Southern California	175
Northwestern University	168
Iowa State College	145
Oberlin College	135

What was the impact of these American-educated scholars on China? By the second decade of this century, a Chinese who earned a degree abroad could use it as a key to official status comparable to the highest of degrees obtained through China's ancient examination system (abolished in 1905). American-trained Chinese composed about one-sixth of the Chinese government officials of cabinet rank in 1915, and about one-fifth in 1937. Some of these, as well as some American-trained Chinese officials in the lower echelons (for example, departments under the ministries or bureaus under the provincial governments) were corrupt bureaucrats of the worst type. Of course there were also American-trained personnel in the Chinese government who fully justified their education. In the middle 1930's, such ministries as railways, communications, health, and foreign affairs, such financial institutions as the Bank of China and the Postal Bank of Savings and Remittance, and such special agencies as the National Resources Commission, employed many Western-trained experts and administrators. Although they had little say as to the major policies of the Nanking government, their effort represented much of its real achievement.

American-trained personnel contributed to Chinese industrial enterprises, both government and private. In 1944, of thirty engineers who held executive position in government-sponsored enterprises, at least thirteen were trained in the United States. In China's private industry, there were such cases as that of Mu Ou-ch'u, who studied cotton farming at a Southern college before the First World War and returned to become a successful manager of cotton mills in Shanghai; of Hu Kuang-piao, a graduate of M.I.T., who in 1932 founded the West China Development Co. in his native Szechwan; and of Hou Te-pang, who studied at M.I.T. and Columbia and in the middle 1930's was a leading executive in the largest chemical works in China. Many more examples await research.

The American-trained students' greatest contribution

to China was probably in the field of education. As scientists, teachers, scholars, and academic administrators, they exerted a fundamental influence beyond their immediate services to government and industry. By the 1930's, the America-returned scholars dominated Chinese college teaching. In the Christian colleges, Chinese scholars who had done graduate work abroad were taking over courses formerly given by Americans. In the leading government and non-Christian private universities, America-returned scholars often made up more than 60 percent of the senior faculty (professors and associate professors). These scholars edited China's new academic journals in science or the humanities and even magazines of ideas and opinion. Although after 1927 the Kuomintang made an increasing effort to inculcate the ideas of Sun Yat-sen and Chiang Kai-shek in Chinese youth, for a decade the government's top educational administrators (including those at the ministry of education as well as those in the provincial bureaus of education) were mostly Western-trained men, many of them having attended the Columbia of John Dewey.

In scientific research and teaching, the American-trained scholars made a signal contribution. For, although before 1941 comparatively few Chinese pursued advanced graduate studies in pure sciences at American universities (earning a total of only 175 Ph.D.'s in the four fields of chemistry, biochemistry, physics, and mathematics), most of them upon their return to China taught and pursued research in Chinese academic institutions such as Tsing Hua, National Peking University, National Central University, or the Academia Sinica. By the 1930's, some of these men were publishing internationally recognized contributions based on work done in China — for

example, Wu Hsien (Ph.D., Harvard, 1919), in the field
of protein research; Sah Peng-t'ieh (Peter Sah; Ph.D.,
Wisconsin, 1926), on synthesized chemical compounds;
and Wu Yu-hsün (Woo Yui-hsun; Ph.D., Chicago, 1925),
on X-ray scattering problems. In the late 1930's students
and assistants trained by these men were publishing significant articles in Chinese scientific journals. Through
those students who became teachers in Chinese middle
schools, the influence of American education spread far
and wide.

In the schools of technology especially the most effective professors were usually American-trained — notably
at Tsing Hua and at Chiao-t'ung, the two best institutions for this kind of training. American education thus
contributed in bringing into being the body of technical
personnel needed for China's industrialization.

Like the scientists and engineers, American-educated
scholars in the humanities and social sciences helped to
raise the level of research and teaching in their fields. But
they performed even more valuable service in disseminat-
ing new ideas and values. It was while he was a student
in the United States that the late Dr. Hu Shih (B.A.,
Cornell, 1915; Ph.D., Columbia, 1917) first conceived the
idea of substituting the vernacular for classical Chinese.
Hu's articles, published in the *Hsin ch'ing-nien* (New
Youth) magazine in Peking in 1917, initiated a literary
revolution. In subsequent years, as a professor at National
Peking University, he inspired new inquiry into China's
heritage through criticism of hitherto unquestioned texts.
Hu also wrote prolifically on Henrik Ibsen, Thomas
Huxley, and John Dewey. He urged Chinese youth to
develop their full capacities as individuals and to question
authority; he helped to popularize the scientific method

and the pragmatic approach to China's problems. His writings were widely available (some of them being reprinted in middle-school textbooks) and had great influence on an entire generation.

American-trained scholars developed the social sciences in China. Western government, economics, and sociology were ably taught in colleges and universities. Such knowledge was also disseminated through magazines eagerly read by middle-school students, even if in their "civics" courses, the *San Min Chu I* (The Three People's Principles) were taught. The American-educated professors pioneered in applying social-science techniques to Chinese subjects — for example, the statistical research done at the Nankai Institute of Economics under the direction of Franklin L. Ho (Ph.D., Yale, 1926), and the sociological surveys done by scholars at Tsing Hua and Yenching under Ch'en Ta (Ph.D., Columbia, 1923) and Wu Wen-tsao (Ph.D., Columbia, 1929). By the 1930's, there was a belated but increasing interest among American-trained scholars concerning rural economic and social problems, and pioneering work such as that of Fei Hsiao-t'ung (a student at Yenching who later studied in Britain) was being prepared.

Although the America-returned scholars made their greatest contribution in the field of education, they also represented a liberal political influence — one which was never fully developed. From the days of the May Fourth Movement in 1919, American-educated scholars were in the forefront among champions of civil rights and critics of government policies. They protested against the warlords and the Kuomintang alike. In 1920, a "Manifesto for the Struggle for Freedom" was signed by Hu Shih, Chiang Meng-lin (Monlin Chiang; B.A., California, 1912;

Ph.D., Columbia, 1917), and others. After 1928, when the Kuomintang extended its control to North China, the Peking professors, although still preoccupied with such subjects as symbolism in poetry, initiated a spirited debate on civil and political liberties. In 1932, Hu Shih and others founded the *Tu-li p'ing-lun* (Independent Critic), which advocated constitutionalism and offered constructive but unrelenting criticism of the government's domestic and foreign policies. During the war, this spirit was kept alive by the *Chin-jih p'ing-lun* (Today's Critic), founded in 1939 by Ch'ien Tuan-sheng (Ph.D., Harvard, 1924) and other professors at the refugee universities at Kunming.

To some American visitors in wartime China, it seemed that American influences were best represented not only by such professors, who kept up political criticism, but also by a unique rural educator then heading a small school for orphans in Chungking. T'ao Hsing-chih was a graduate of a missionary school and, in 1914, got his B.A. degree at a Christian college—Nanking University. In 1915 he went to the United States on borrowed funds, and for the next two years studied educational philosophy at Columbia with John Dewey. In 1927, ten years after he returned to China, he founded a highly successful "rural normal school" at Hsiao-chuang, near Nanking, but it was closed by the government in 1930. Later he founded in Shanghai the "little teacher movement" — a system under which each student was made responsible for teaching other persons to read. After the outbreak of the war against Japan, T'ao's disciples continued the movement in Kwangsi, Hunan, and other provinces. But its rapid growth again aroused the government's suspicion, and the system was suppressed. Until his death in 1946,

T'ao believed that his own educational philosophy was an outgrowth of Deweyism — stressing "the unity of teaching, learning and doing" in a Chinese environment.

These examples of individual achievement suggest the rich possibilities for biographical research on persons who really belonged in some degree to two cultures and who contributed to China's modernization in ways not yet studied nor adequately appreciated. Their story may be the most important part of any account of the bygone era of American influence in China.

Today, this record of Chinese who once sojourned in the United States and of Americans who resided in China seems a matter of the remote past. American traders who dealt in silk, wood oil, kerosene, cigarettes, or machinery have long since left the China coast, while the missionaries, driven from their adopted homes, have found new fields in Taiwan and other East Asian lands. In the militant Communist state that arose in mainland China few could recognize any traces of American influence.

Yet the United States today, as in the past, faces the problem of American influence in Asia — still a frontier of cultural as well as political contact. In the form of foreign aid, and with entirely new motives, American capital continues to be exported to Asia; in the Peace Corps and in the numerous projects of philanthropic and academic institutions a new kind of missionary has emerged; and Asian students continue to visit our shores. As we face the difficulties of today, we may gain from a knowledge of the past. This essay has presented in outline the past relations between Americans and a major Asian people. It remains for the historian to determine the exact extent and the effects, for better or worse, of

American influences upon China and the Chinese. I hope that the questions of fact and interpretation raised in this survey — and the wealth of available material indicated by the following bibliography — may stimulate scholarly investigation which is urgently needed and long overdue.

II

BIBLIOGRAPHICAL
SUGGESTIONS

ABBREVIATIONS

The following abbreviations were used for the 82 libraries and other institutions where manuscript sources germane to American-Chinese relations are to be found.

ABFMS   American Baptist Foreign Mission Society, 475 Riverside Drive, New York 27, New York (write to ABHS)

ABHS   American Baptist Historical Society, 1100 South Goodman Street, Rochester 20, New York

ABS   American Bible Society, 450 Park Avenue, New York 22, New York

ARC   American National Red Cross, 18th and D Streets, N.W., Washington 6, D.C.

ASSUL   American Sunday School Union Library, 1816 Chestnut Street, Philadelphia 3, Pennsylvania.

BA   Boston Athenaeum, 101/2 Beacon Street, Boston, Massachusetts

BPL   Boston Public Library, Boston, Massachusetts

BHA   Belchertown Historical Association, Belchertown, Massachusetts

Bel.C   Beloit College, Beloit, Wisconsin

Br.U   Brown University, John Carter Brown Library, Providence 12, Rhode Island

CBL   College of the Bible Library, Lexington, Kentucky

CHS   California Historical Society, 2090 Jackson Street, San Francisco 9, California

CMBNY   China Medical Board of New York, 30 East 60th Street, New York, New York

CUL:EA   Columbia University Libraries: East Asian Library, New York 27, New York

CUL:SC	Columbia University Libraries: Special Collections, New York 27, New York
Ch.HS	Church Historical Society, 606 Rathervue Place, Austin, Texas
Cor.U	Cornell University, Collection of Regional History and Cornell University Archives, Ithaca, New York
DHS	Disciples Historical Society, 1101 19th Avenue South, Nashville 12, Tennessee
DUL	Duke University Library, Durham, North Carolina
EI	Essex Institute, 132 Essex Street, Salem, Massachusetts
EUL	Emory University Library, Atlanta 22, Georgia
FDRL	Franklin D. Roosevelt Library, Hyde Park, New York
FUL	Fisk University Library, Nashville 8, Tenneesee
GCL	Girard College Library, Corinthian and Girard Avenues, Philadelphia 21, Pennsylvania
HSTL	Harry S. Truman Library, Independence, Missouri
HU:AAGH	Harvard University: Arnold Arboretum and Gray Herbarium, 22 Divinity Avenue, Cambridge 38, Massachusetts
HU:BL	Harvard University: Baker Library, Graduate School of Business Administration, Boston 63, Massachusetts
HU:CJL	Harvard University: Chinese-Japanese Library, 2 Divinity Avenue, Cambridge 38, Massachusetts
HU:HL	Harvard University: Houghton Library, Cambridge 38, Massachusetts
HU:LC	Harvard University: Littauer Center, Cambridge 38, Massachusetts
HU:SMPHL	Harvard University: Schools of Medicine and Public Health Library, Harvard Medical School, Boston, Massachusetts

HU:WL	Harvard University: Widener Library, Cambridge 38, Massachusetts
Hav.CL	Haverford College Library, Haverford, Pennsylvania
Hunt.L	Henry E. Huntington Library and Art Gallery, San Marino, California
JHU	The Johns Hopkins University, Baltimore 18, Maryland
LC	Library of Congress, Washington 25, D.C.
LCP	Library Company of Philadelphia, Broad and Christian Streets, Philadelphia 47, Pennsylvania
MC:DWM	Methodist Church: Division of World Missions, 475 Riverside Drive, New York 27, New York
MF	The Information Bureau, The Maryknoll Fathers, Maryknoll, New York
MHS	Massachusetts Historical Society, 1154 Boylston Street, Boston 15, Massachusetts
MM	Mariners Museum, Newport News, Virginia
MRC	George C. Marshall Research Center, P.O. Box 831, Lexington, Virginia
MRL	Missionary Research Library, 3041 Broadway, New York 27, New York
Mich.U	University of Michigan, Ann Arbor, Michigan
Minn.HS	Minnesota Historical Society, St. Paul 1, Minnesota
Mo.U	University of Missouri Library, Columbia, Missouri
NBTSL	New Brunswick Theological Seminary Library, New Brunswick, New Jersey
NCPEC	National Council of the Protestant Episcopal Church, Overseas Department, 281 Park Avenue South, New York 10, New York
NCUL	University of North Carolina Library, Chapel Hill, North Carolina
NFTC	National Foreign Trade Council, 111 Broadway, New York, New York

NHHS	New Hampshire Historical Society, 30 Park Street, Concord, New Hampshire
NHS	Nevada State Historical Society, P.O. Box 1129, Reno, Nevada
NJHS	New Jersey Historical Society, 230 Broadway, Newark 4, New Jersey
NYHS	New York Historical Society, 170 Central Park West, New York 24, New York
NYPL	New York Public Library, Fifth Avenue and 42nd Street, New York 18, New York
OUL	University of Oregon Library, Eugene, Oregon
PBFM	United Presbyterian Church in the U.S.A., Board of Foreign Missions Archives, Room 1056, 475 Riverside Drive, New York 27, New York
PHS	Historical Society of Pennsylvania, 1300 Locust Street, Philadelphia 7, Pennsylvania
PIA	Princeton in Asia, 475 Riverside Drive, New York 27, New York
PMS	Peabody Museum of Salem, Essex Street, Salem, Massachusetts
PRC:HF	Historical Foundation of the Presbyterian and Reformed Churches, Montreat, North Carolina
PSRL	Pacific School of Religion Library, 1798 Scenic Avenue, Berkeley 9, California
Pr.HS	Presbyterian Historical Society, 520 Witherspoon Building, Juniper and Walnut Streets, Philadelphia 7, Pennsylvania
RIHS	Rhode Island Historical Society, 52 Power Street, Providence 6, Rhode Island
RUL	Rutgers University Library, New Brunswick, New Jersey
SBC:FMB	Southern Baptist Convention: Foreign Mission Board, 2037 Monument Avenue, Richmond 20, Virginia
SCWL	State College of Washington Library, Pullman, Washington
SU	Stanford University, Stanford, California

Syr.U	Syracuse University, Syracuse 10, New York
Trin.CL	Trinity College Library, Hartford 6, Connecticut
UBCHEA	United Board for Christian Higher Education in Asia, 475 Riverside Drive, New York 27, New York
UCB:BL	University of California, Berkeley: Bancroft Library, Berkeley 4, California
UCB:GL	University of California, Berkeley: General Library, Berkeley 4, California
US:AF	United States: Air Force, Historical Division, Maxwell Air Force Base, Alabama
US:NA	United States: National Archives, Washington 25, D.C.
US:ND	United States: Navy Department, Naval History Division, Office of the Chief of Naval Operations, Washington 25, D.C.
Urs.CL	Ursinus College Library, Collegeville, Pennsylvania
VUL	University of Virginia Library, Charlottesville, Virginia
WUL	University of Washington Library, Seattle 5, Washington
YMCA:HL	Historical Library of the YMCA, National Board of YMCA's, 291 Broadway, New York, New York
YU:DL	Yale University: Divinity Library, New Haven, Connecticut
YU:SL	Yale University: Sterling Memorial Library, New Haven, Connecticut

1. MANUSCRIPTS AND ARCHIVES

Most of the 455 entries in this chapter were found in libraries and depositories in the Boston area, New Haven, New York, and Washington. Others were located through correspondence and from various guides and inventories, especially Philip M. Hamer's invaluable *A Guide to Archives and Manuscripts in the United States* (New Haven, 1961). The reader is urged to consult this volume and other guides to manuscripts and archives (full lists of which are given in Hamer), as well as the Library of Congress' *The National Union Catalog of Manuscript Collections, 1959–1961* (Ann Arbor, 1962). When planning research it is advisable to write to the library or depository concerned, as access to manuscript collections and archives is often restricted to those who have obtained written permission.

1.1 MERCHANTS, ENTREPRENEURS, AND ENGINEERS

Appleton family. Appleton Papers. 25 vols. of correspondence, etc., of Nathan Appleton, Sr., Nathan Appleton, Jr., William Sumner Appleton, *et al.* 1775–1890, MHS

Astor, John Jacob. Papers. 19 vols. and 35 boxes. 1784–1892. HU:BL

Astor, John Jacob. Papers. 1 box, including letters on the fur trade. 1792–1843. NYPL

Ayers, Howard. Memorandum on Trade between the United States and China, 1840–1910, with particular reference to cotton cloth, etc. 20 pp., typewritten. NYPL

Bancroft, George, comp. Bancroft Collection. 416 vols. Materials up to 1883. NYPL

Bancroft, Hubert H., comp. Solid Men of Boston in the Northwest: Material from the Bancroft Collection, Berkeley, California. MHS

Barker, Wharton. Papers. 12 vols. and 27 boxes, including correspondence on investments in China and Russia. 1870–1920. LC

Beebe, Charles E. *See* Abiel Abbot Low.

Blydenburgh, William J. (New York and Shanghai). 3 letterbooks. 1864–1876. HU:BL

Boardman, William H., Jr. (Boston). Papers. 2 vols. 1824–1829. HU:BL

Boit, John. Complete narrative of second voyage of the *Columbia.* MHS

Boit, John. Sea Journal. 1790–1806. MHS

Bool, Henry W. *See* Isaac Clason.

Brewer, Henry. Journal of a journey to China. 310 pp. 1897. YU:SL

Brown family. Papers. 300,000 pieces, including materials on early China trade. 1750–1900. Br.U.

Bryant, John. 2 account books. 1801–1812. HU:BL

Cabot, Samuel. Papers. 1 vol. and 3 boxes, including materials on the China trade. 1713–1859. MHS

Carrington family. Papers. About 400 vols. and 300 boxes, including considerable material on the China trade. 18th and 19th centuries. RIHS

Cary, Thomas Greaves. Clipper Ships and the China Trade, etc. 1 vol. BA

Clark, Robert J. Arthur Hamilton Clark. 62 pp., type-written. (Contains material on Capt. Clark's experiences in China.) PMS and MM

Clason, Isaac. Articles of agreement between Isaac Clason, owner of ship *Frances-Henrietta,* and Henry W. Bool, mariner, to act as master, supercargo and consignee, on voyage to Canton, June 12, 1809. NYHS

Cleveland, Richard J. Manuscripts. PMS

Constable, William. Papers. 25 vols. and 31 boxes, including shipping papers relating to trade with China. 1774–1850. NYPL

Coolidge, Mrs. Joseph. Diaries. 1839. Heard Papers; HU:BL

Cowles, John Phelps, Jr. Letters from China. *See* Markham and Puffer families.

Crowninshield family. Papers. Approximately 2000 items, including materials on trade to the Malay archipelago and the Far East. 1789–1895. EI

Cushing, John P. Diary. 4 vols. 1834–1840, 1850–1856. BA

Cushing, John P. Papers. 6 vols. and 1 box. 1832–1882. HU:BL

Delano, Edward. Diary. 40 vols. 1838–1859. The volumes for 1841–1849 are available also in typescript (made at the order of F. D. Roosevelt, probably in 1913–1920). Also account books. 1852–1882. FDRL

Derby, Elias Hasket. Receipts and bills. 1787–1793. EI

Derby family. Commercial papers. 34 vols., 4 boxes, and 1 envelope. 1715–1858. EI

Dorr, Sullivan (Canton and Boston). 2 letterbooks and 1 account book. 1799–1808. HU:BL

Dorr, Sullivan (Boston, China, and Providence). Papers. 1 box (typewritten material collected by H. Corning). EI

Edgar, William. Papers. 11 vols., including letters on the China trade. 1750–1870. NYPL

Emery, Noah, Jr. Invoice of merchandise shipped by him and Augustine Heard, for *William*. 1809. Henry Wheatland Papers, vol. 5, EI

Flemming, Sampson. Letterbook, including letters to William Edgar (New York), relating to ships *Empress of China* and *Edgar*. 1782–1790. NYPL

Forbes, John Murray. Family letters bearing dates 1808 to 1902. MHS

Forbes, John Murray. Journals, letterbooks, etc. 1829– . Forbes Collection; HU:BL

Forbes, John Murray. Letters (mainly to P. S. Forbes). Typewritten volume. 1843–1867. HU:BL

Forbes, Paul Sieman. Accounts and letters. 1825–1886. Forbes Collection; HU:BL

Forbes, Paul Sieman. Papers. Especially letters received by P. S. Forbes. Forbes Collection; HU:BL

Forbes, Robert Bennet. Account books and letters. 1825– . Forbes Collection; HU:BL

Forbes, Thomas T. Letterbooks and accounts, etc. 1822–1828. Forbes Collection; HU:BL

Forbes, William Cameron. Journals. 10 vols. 1904–1913, 1914–1946. MHS (duplicates in HU:HL)

Forbes, William Cameron. Papers. 200 vols. and 20 boxes. 1870–1950. HU:HL

Forbes, William Cameron. Papers. A variety of business records. Forbes Collection; HU:BL

Forbes family. Papers. 50 vols., 5 boxes, and 5 cases. 1803–1920. Forbes Collection; HU:BL

Girard, Stephen. Papers. More than 100,000 letters and

many boxes of uncatalogued material. 1772–1831. GCL

Girard, Stephen. Papers. 1 box. 1794–1811. PHS

E. H. Green vs. Estate of Jonathan Russell, Boston and Manila. 4 boxes. 1868–1886. HU:BL

Grew, Henry (Boston). Account book. 1851–1862. HU:BL

Grew, Henry. Papers. 7 boxes. 1801–1865. MHS

Griswold, George. *See* Illinois Central Railroad Company.

Griswold, William Frederick. Sea journal. 1834–1835. YU:SL

Haswell, Robert. Logs of first and second voyages of the *Columbia.* 1787–1790, 1790–1793. MHS

Heard, Augustine. Diaries. 1831–1839. Heard Papers; HU:BL

Heard, Augustine. *See* Noah Emery, Jr.

Heard, Augustine, Jr. Miscellaneous writings containing reminiscences on China and Japan. 4 items, typewritten. Heard Papers: HU:BL

Heard, George W. Journal. 1859. EI

Heard, John, III. Diaries. 1839, 1849–1860, 1861–1863. Heard Papers; HU:BL

Heard, John, III. Memoirs. Typewritten. Heard Papers; HU:BL

Heard family (Ipswich, Mass.). Papers. 800 vols., 272 boxes, and 103 cases. 1754–1898. HU:BL

Heard family. Letters and diaries. 1 envelope containing letters, 1822–1879; 1 box containing letters, 1859–1875, and diaries (mostly typewritten copies). EI

Higginson, Henry Lee. Papers. About 70 boxes and 3 cartons. 1870–1918. HU:BL

Hill, Samuel. Autobiography, including account of experiences on Northwest Coast and in China. Dated 1819. 42 pp. NYPL

Hill, Samuel. Journal and log of two voyages: the *Ophelia* from Boston to Chile and China, 1815–1817; and the *Packet* from Boston to Chile and China, 1817–1820. 352 pp. and 15 plates. NYPL

Hill, Samuel. 2 letters, to Bryant and Sturgis, Boston, Feb. 28, 1817, and to J. P. Cushing, March 8, 1823. MHS

Hollingsworth, Levi. Papers. PHS

Hoskins, John B. Narrative of second voyage of the *Columbia*. MHS

Hunnewell, James. Papers. 2 boxes. 1829–1871. MHS

Hunnewell family (mainly James) (Charlestown, Boston, and Honolulu). Papers. 83 bundles and 17 cases. 1823–1869. HU:BL

Hunnewell family and firm. Papers. 15 vols. and 16 boxes. 1809–1879. HU:BL

Hunt, Thomas Franklin, comp. Collection of newspaper clippings upon China and the Chinese. 17 vols. EI

Hunter, William C. Journal of Occurrences during Cessation of Trade at Canton. 37 pp. May 1839. BA

Ingersoll, Nathaniel. Accounts of sales of sundries; bill of lading, signed by Ingersoll, for *Ganges*, Salem. 1809. EI

Ingraham, Joseph. Journal of the voyage of the brigantine *Hope* from Boston to the Northwest Coast of America. 1790–1792. LC

Kinsman, Nathaniel. Bills, receipts, etc. 1 box. 1750–1799. EI

Kinsman family. Papers. 5 vols., including Nathaniel Kinsman's letters from China, 1818–1847; other materials covering the period 1794–1878. EI

Latimer family (mainly John R. Latimer). Papers. 7 vols. and 43 boxes, 1679–1892 (mostly 1821–1834). LC

Leaming family. Papers. Approximately 5000 items. 1706–1861. PHS

Low, Abiel Abbot. Papers. 7 boxes, including materials relating to trade with China and Japan. 1829–1873. LC

Low, Abiel Abbot. Tribute to the memory of Charles E. Beebe, tea merchant of New York (letter to Mr. Barret). Sept. 20, 1892. NYHS

Low, Abiel Abbot and Seth. Bills of lading, etc. 1834–1875. NYPL

Low, Edward Allen. China Trade Papers. 1 folder. 1842–1849. Low Family Papers; LC

Low, Josiah O. Papers. Letters received from William H. Low (Canton, Macao, etc.). 58 pieces. 1837–1842. NYPL

Low, William. Papers. 2 boxes, including correspondence and accounts while in China as agent for Minturn and Champlain, 1815–1817. 1808–1817. NYPL

Low, William H. See Josiah O. Low.

Low family. Papers. Including the papers of several members of the family, such as Abiel Abbot Low, Harriet Low, and Edward Allen Low. In addition, there is a collection of family papers on the China trade in 16 boxes and 2 folders. 1806–1930. LC

Markham and Puffer families. Correspondence and other papers, including letters from John Phelps Cowles, Jr., written in China. 1853–1907. Cor.U

Morris, Robert. Private letterbooks. 2 vols. 1794–1798. LC

Neal, David A. (Salem). Papers. 14 vols. 1818–1877. HU:BL

Newton, Benjamin (Boston, Canton, and Singapore). Papers. 5 boxes. 1843–1864. HU:BL

Nichols, J. Howard (Boston and China). Papers. 4 vols. and 1 case. 1856–1905. HU:BL

Nye, Gideon, Jr. (Macao and Canton). Papers. 2 vols. (day books) and 1 envelope of miscellaneous papers. 1858–1898. HU:BL

Oliver, Francis J. Papers. Heard Papers; HU:BL

Olyphant, D. W. C. (Canton and Shanghai). Selected letters, 1 package, typewritten; copy made under the supervision of D. W. Lyon. 1827–1851. MRL

Page, Benjamin. Promissory note to Samqua (to pay $3593.37 in 20 mos.), Dec. 20, 1796; receipt signed Ponqua. NYHS

Parsons, William Barclay. Papers. 12 bundles. 1881–1900. NYPL

Parsons, William Barclay. Papers. 1 box. 1899–1915. CUL:SC

Peabody, George. Papers. 140 boxes and many letters and account books. Chiefly 1830–1857. EI

Peabody, Joseph. Certificate of tea imported by Joseph Peabody in the ship *Sumatra* from Canton. 1 envelope. 1829. EI

Peabody, Joseph L. Papers. MHS

Peele, Willard. Papers. Approximately 375 items, including materials on the trade with Batavia and the Far East. 1818–1863. EI

Perkins, Thomas Handasyd. Papers. 33 vols. and 4 boxes. 1773–1853. MHS

Phillips family. Papers. Approximately 6000 items, including materials on the Sumatra trade and some Chinese ports. 1796–1886. EI

Puffer family. *See* Markham and Puffer families.

Rulon, John W. Papers. Approximately 3000 items. 1807–1861. PHS

Russell, Jonathan. *See* E. H. Green vs. Estate of Jonathan Russell.

Russell, Samuel. Papers. 21 boxes. Mostly 1812–1849. LC

Sands, George U. Papers. 16 vols. and 2 boxes. 1866–1879. HU:BL

Shaw, Samuel (Canton), letter to John Hancock. Dec. 1790. BPL

Silsbee, Nathaniel. Papers. 2 vols., 1 box, and 1 portfolio. Letters, 1799–1844; other family papers, 1637–1888. EI

Smith, Thomas H. (New York). Account books. 1823. NYHS

Steward, Ira W. (associated with John Caswell & Co.). Letters. 1 vol. 1869–1881. NYPL

Sturgis, Jonathan. *See* Illinois Central Railroad Company.

Sturgis, William. Logbooks and manuscript lecture notes on the voyages of *Eliza* (1798–1799), *Pearl* (1805–1806), and *Atahualpa* (1811–1816). MHS

Sturgis, William. Papers. 3 vols. and 1 box. 1798–1816. MHS

Taylor, Moses (New York). Papers. 1100 vols. and 53 cases. 1832–1888. NYPL

Thomas, James Augustus. Papers. 28,485 items, including materials on the tobacco business in China. 1905–1941. DUL

Tilden, Bryant Parrott. Journals. Many volumes. 1815–1837. (Typed copy available.) PMS

Tingey, Thomas, to Williangs [*sic*] & Francis, Phila. Dec. 4, 1795. Letter on Eastern markets, etc., written in Calcutta. NYHS

Waldo, Charles Frederick. Remarks on a voyage from Boston to Canton in the ship *Indus,* 1802–1803. EI

Waln, Robert. Papers. Approximately 500 items, most of

which relate to the East India and China trade. 1792–1823. PHS

Waln family. Papers. 25 vols. 1784–1823. LCP

Waters family. Papers. Approximately 20,000 items, including materials on Sumatran, Chinese, and Philippine trades. 1695–1913. EI

Wheatland, Richard. Bill of lading and other papers of goods on board *Indus*, Boston. 1802. Henry Wheatland Papers; EI

Wigglesworth, Thomas (Boston). Papers. 12 vols. of letterbooks, etc. 1806–1847. HU:BL

Williams, Charles H. Journal of a voyage from Boston to Batavia, Canton, etc. April 16, 1836 — Dec. 17, 1837. EI

Williams, Franklin Delano. Letters written in China to his wife. 1854–1857, 1861–1865. PMS

Wilson, James Harrison. Papers. 13 vols. and 76 boxes. 1861–1920. LC

Wolcott, Frederick Henry. Diary. 2 vols. 1849–1854. NYPL

Woodward, Marcus L. Diary, kept on board ship *Surprise*, owned by A. A. Low & Brothers. 1 vol. 1861. NYHS

1.2 BUSINESS FIRMS

American Fur Co. Papers. 131 vols. and 53 boxes. 1831–1847. NYHS

American Fur Co. and Pacific Fur Co. Papers. 16 vols. and 29 boxes, including materials on the China trade. HU:BL

William Appleton & Co. Papers. 87 vols. and 93 boxes, including papers of Samuel Hooper & Co. 1840–1889. HU:BL

Boston Marine Insurance Co. Records. MHS

British–American Tobacco Co. *See* James Augustus Thomas.

Brown and Ives (Providence). Papers. Br.U

Brown and Ives. *Anne and Hope,* Christopher Bentley. Disbursements while on three voyages to London and Canton. 1801. Brown and Ives Papers; Br.U

Brown and Ives. *John Jay.* Account book. 1798. Brown and Ives Papers; Br.U

Bryant and Sturgis (Boston). Papers. 13 vols. and 1 box. 1812–1872. HU:BL

China and Japan Trading Co. *See* Fogg Brothers

Commercial Insurance Co. (Boston). Papers. 1 vol. 1812–1813. HU:BL

Dane, Dana & Co. (Boston). Papers. 24 boxes and 2 cases. 1851–1859. HU:BL

Thomas and William Davis (Plymouth, Mass.). Papers. 7 boxes. 1782–1805. HU:BL

Dutilh and Wacksmuth (Philadelphia). Business papers. 2 boxes and 1 portfolio. 1784–1797. LC

Electric Boat Co. (Groton, Conn.). Letters between the Company and their agent in Peking. 1 box. 1910–1923. HU:BL

Ephraim and James Emerton (Salem). Papers. 5 vols. and 1 box. 1816–1835. HU:BL

Fanning, Edmund. List of teas imported by Edmund Fanning in ship *Teaplant,* Peter Murphy, master, from Canton. October 27, 1812. Misc. Mss.; NYHS

Fogg Brothers (Boston). Papers, etc. 300 pieces, relating to China trade, particularly cotton cloth. 1847–1926. NYPL

Forbes-Perkins & Co. (Boston). Papers. Those concerning the China trade deal with the period around 1920. Forbes Collection; HU:BL

Franklin [N.H.] Nail Works. Papers. 1836–1847. Heard Papers; HU:BL

Edward Goold & Co. (New York). 1 letterbook, including letters to New England merchants relating to trade with Europe, India, and China. 1797–1798. NYPL

Gouverneur and Kemble (New York). Letterbook, containing correspondence relative to ships sent to West Indies, Europe, and China. 626 pp. 1796–1798. NYPL

S. Griffitts Morgan (San Francisco). Papers. 19 vols. and 27 boxes. 1843–1863. HU:BL

Augustine Heard & Co. *See* Heard family.

Samuel Hooper & Co. (Boston). *See* William Appleton & Co.

James Houghton & Co. Papers. 1839–1847. Heard Papers; HU:BL

Howland & Aspinwall (New York). Papers. 37 vols. and 52 boxes; part of the Comstock Brothers papers. 1833–1876. HU:BL

Thomas Hunt & Co. (Hongkong). Papers. 25 vols. 1863–1869. HU:BL

Illinois Central Railroad Company. Papers. 16 vols. and 5 boxes, including material on Jonathan Sturgis and George Griswold. 1846–1898. HU:BL

Indusco. Chinese Industrial Cooperatives (Indusco) files. 11 shelves. 1938–1948. CUL:EA

Ipswich Cotton Mills. Papers. 1847–1861. Heard Papers; HU:BL

Ipswich Manufacturing Co. Papers. 1828–1864. Heard Papers; HU:BL

Ipswich Manufacturing Co. Papers. David Pingree Papers; EI

J. and T. Lamb (Boston). Lamb Papers. Correspondence and business records. 1815–1865. MHS

Loring Brothers Co. (Boston and Valparaiso). Papers. 5 vols. and 1 box. 1834–1858. HU:BL

Miscellaneous papers dealing with East India trade. 6 boxes. 1800–1880. RIHS

Miscellaneous shipping and commercial papers, including occasional documents on Sumatran and Chinese trade. 1695–1870. EI

National Foreign Trade Council. Archives, including records of American trade with China. NFTC

Pacific Fur Co. *See* American Fur Co.

Pacific Mail Steamship Co. Records. 550 vols. and 190,000 pieces. 1853–1917. Hunt.L.

Pepperell Manufacturing Co. Papers. Approximately 1000 vols., 22 boxes, and 73 cases. Chiefly 1839–1928. HU:BL

Perkins & Co. (Canton). Papers. 25 vols. and 1 case, including papers of Russell & Co. (Canton). 1820–1891. HU:BL

Perkins & Co. Letters. 1838. Forbes Collection; HU:BL

J. and T. H. Perkins (Boston). Account books. 20 vols. 1804–1836. MHS

Roxbury Land Co. (Roxbury, Mass.). Papers. 1836–1868. Heard Papers; HU:BL

Russell & Co. *See* Forbes family.

Russell & Co. (Canton). Papers. 15 vols. 1867–1881. HU:BL

Samuel Russell & Co. Papers. Invoice books, day-books, journals and accounts, miscellaneous papers, and 2 letterbooks. 1819–1823. Samuel Russell Papers; LC

Silsbee, Pickman & Allen (Salem, Mass.). Papers. 75 vols. and unbound papers. 1843–1893. EI

Standard Oil Co. (New Jersey). Export Trade Record. Contains materials on China to 1911. *See* Ralph W.

Hidy and Muriel E. Hidy, *Pioneering in Big Business,
1882–1911* (New York, 1955).

Steward & Jones. Letterbooks. 1786–1795. NYHS

Nathan Trotter & Co. (Philadelphia). Papers. 1172 vols.,
160 boxes, 4 cases, and 25 crates, including material
on China trade in early nineteenth century. 1798–1918.
HU:BL

J. and R. Waln. Letterbooks, accounts, etc. Ridgeway
Branch; LCP

Wolcott, Oliver. 2 account books of his business in New
York, including trade with China. 1804–1815. NYHS

Wolcott, Oliver. Letterbook of Oliver Wolcott & Co.,
1803–1805, and of Oliver Wolcott, 1805–1808. Contains records of fur and tea trades with Canton. NYPL

1.3 MISSIONARIES

Abeel, David. Amoy journal. 1 vol. 1842–1843. Canton
journal. 1 vol. 1839–1840. Journey to China. 1 vol.
1838–1839. Sermons, letters, journal, etc. 1 basket
stored in vault. NBTSL

Allen, Young J. Papers. 700 pieces. 1857–1907. EUL

Anonymous. Account of the Japanese Atrocities at Nanking. Introductory note by John LeRoy Christian. 24
pp., typewritten. 1937–1938. HU:HL

Ashmore, William. Newspaper articles (indexed scrapbook). 1868–1879. MRL

Bashford, James W. Diaries. 54 vols. (nos. 18–19 missing).
1904–1918. MRL

Blodget, Henry. Sermon by Rev. Henry Blodget of
Peking. 1866. ABCFM Papers; HU:HL

Boynton, Charles L. Collection of Christian Life and
Work. Numerous looseleaf binders and notebooks on

missionary biographies as well as mimeographed and other material of the National Christian Council. Data on missionaries under individual societies. 8 looseleaf binders. Missionary biographies. 7 looseleaf binders. MRL

Bradley, Charles William. Notes on Chinese Religion, Law, Higher Institutions of Learning, Government, Literature, Social Life and Customs, etc., part of a MS, about 200 pp. YU:SL

Bridgman, Elijah C. Papers. Approximately 80 items. 1820–1839. BHA

Burgess, John Stewart. Materials on Peking student work. 1 box. 1911–1921. YMCA:HL

Cheng Ching-yi. Manuscript material on Dr. Cheng Ching-yi from John R. Mott. MRL

Condit, Ira M. Journal, Canton, 1865–   . Presbyterian China Archives, Index vol. 7; PBFM

Corbett, Hunter. Extracts from Journal covering Seven Months' Work. 1869. Presbyterian China Archives, Index vol. 9; PBFM

Dickinson, James Taylor. Chinese and English Vocabularies. 284 pp. YU:SL

Dodd, Samuel. Journal. 1861–1877. 315 pp., typewritten. MRL

Doty, Elihu. Journal written in Batavia, Singapore, Borneo, and Amoy, China. 1836–1845. Abeel Papers; NBTSL

Doty-Dubois family. Papers. Correspondence of Rev. Elihu Doty and his daughter, Amelia C. Doty Dubois. 1846–1865. NYPL

Gayley, S. R. My First Twelve Months in Tung Chau [Tungchow]. Written in June 1862. Presbyterian China Archives, Index vol. 5; PBFM

Goucher, John F. Papers. 53 folders. Mainly 1901–1922. MRL

Hartwell, Charles. Diaries. 32 vols. 1850–1905. ABCFM Papers; HU:HL

Hartwell, Hannah Louisa Peet. Teacher's Notebooks, etc. 1897. YU:SL

Hayes, Paul G. Biographic Records of Chinese Christian and Non-Christian Leaders of the 20th century. 3 looseleaf binders. MRL

Hepburn, J. C. Journal. 1843–1845. Presbyterian China Archives, Index vol. 1; PBFM

Hubbard, Hugh W. Miscellaneous writings. 1930–1931. Diary, 1937–1938. ABCFM Papers; HU:HL

Hume, Edward Hicks. Manuscripts and press articles. 292 items. 1913–1955. MRL

Hume, Edward Hicks. Papers. 2 boxes. 1838–1928. CUL:SC

Jenness, Lillian Holmes. In and Out of the Bamboo Curtain. 42 pp., typewritten. 1937–1951. PBFM

Jones, Catherine Ella. Letters. Walter Jones papers (185 items, 1819–1880). DUL

Lautenschlager, Stanton. Threat of Communism in China. 10 pp., typewritten. Received, 1932. PBFM

Lewis, Spencer. Pioneering in West China. 112 pp. 1939. MRL

Lloyd, John. Journal. 1847– . Presbyterian China Archives, Index vol. 6; PBFM

Lowrie, Walter M. Journal. Aug.-Oct. 1843; 1845–1846. Presbyterian China Archives, Index vols. 1–2; PBFM

Lyon, D. Willard. Papers. At least two filing drawers of correspondence and other material on YMCA work in China up to 1930's. MRL

Martin, William Alexander Parsons. The Peiho and Peking. 2 folders. 1860. PBFM

McCartee, Divie Bethune. Miscellaneous materials. Photographs and biographical sketches. 1 envelope. MRL

Moffet, Anna E. The Nanking Tragedy: A Statement of Personal Experience. 8 pp., typewritten. May 1927. PBFM

Moninger, Margaret M. Letters. 1915–1941. Pr.HS

Mott, John R. Papers. About 45 file drawers of manuscript materials. YU:DL

Porter, Lucius C. Papers, including diaries starting about 1896. 4 file drawers and many boxes. Bel.C

Poteat, Edwin McNeill. Papers. 4000 pieces, including materials for the period when Mr. Poteat was a Baptist missionary in China. 1925–1956. NCUL

Rawlinson, Frank. Miscellaneous papers. 1 package of typewritten manuscripts, etc., covering a period up to 1930's. MRL

Robinson, Arthur G. Papers on YMCA Work in North China, etc. 1913–1937. HU:CJL

Schereschewsky, Samuel I. J., Mrs. Letters. 1 package. Ch.HS

Scott, Charles E. Is the Holy Spirit Dead: The Story of How a Mountain Church Handled Its Murder Case. 1 folder. 1911. PBFM

Scott, Charles E. Sinister Methods in Shantung. 31 pp., typewritten. 1920. YU:SL

Shuck, J. Lewis. Letters. 1 folder. Mainly before 1853. SBC:FMB

Sites, Nathan. Papers. 1 package, including letters and journal. 1860's. MRL

Stauffer, Milton T. Manuscript on David Abeel. 27 pp., typewritten. 1941. NBTSL

Steinbeck, Clark S. Through the Gates. 20 pp., typewritten. 1923. PBFM

Taylor, Joseph. West of the Yangtze Gorges. 153 pp. 1936. PBFM

Thurston, John Lawrence. Correspondence. 1 box. 1894–1904. YU:SL

Tomlin, Olive Bird. 28 letters from China, 1917–1950. YU:SL

Way, R. Q. History of the Ningpo Mission. Oct. 1, 1855. Presbyterian China Archives, Index vol. 4; PBFM

White, Moses Clark. Manuscripts relating to the founding of Methodist missions in Foochow. 110 pp., typewritten. Late 1840's and 1850's. YU:SL

Yates, Matthew T. Ancestor Worship: A Revised Edition of an Essay Read before the Missionary Conference Held at Shanghai, May 10–24, 1877. Shanghai, 1878. MRL

1.4 MISSION SOCIETIES AND CHURCH SERVICE ORGANIZATIONS

American and Foreign Bible Society. Records. ABHS

American Baptist Foreign Mission Society. Missionary correspondence. At least 3 boxes. For the period before 1900. In storage, as of 1961. ABFMS

American Bible Society. Archives going back to 1816, including both foreign and domestic correspondence and minutes of committees. Archives are being microfilmed and partly preserved. ABS

American Board of Commissioners for Foreign Missions. Papers. Covering the period 1812–1952. HU:HL. These papers have a checklist of 109 pp. plus loose leaves. The following divisions are especially pertinent to China:

ABC   16.3.1   Canton Mission
ABC   16.3.3   Amoy Mission; 2 vols.; 1820–1854
ABC   16.3.5   Foochow Mission; 36 vols.; 1860–1927
ABC   16.3.6   Foochow Mission, Women's Board; 7 vols.; 1871–1927
ABC   16.3.7   Foochow Mission, Miscellaneous; 11 vols. and 1 box; 1848–1950
ABC   16.3.8   South China Mission; 7 vols.; 1831–1919
ABC   16.3.9   South China Mission, Treasury Department
ABC   16.3.10 South China Mission, Women's Board
ABC   16.3.11 South China Mission, Miscellaneous
ABC   16.3.12 North China Mission; 88 vols.; 1860–1952
ABC   16.3.13 North China Mission, Women's Board; 8 vols.; 1871–1927
ABC   16.3.14 North China Mission; 8 vols.; 1889–1941
ABC   16.3.15 Shansi Mission; 7 vols.; 1880–1919
ABC   16.3.18 Shaowu Mission; 9 vols.; 1920–1952
American Christian Missionary Society. *See* United Christian Missionary Society.
American Friends Service Committee. Archives. Several hundred cubic feet. 1917 until recent years. Hav.CL
American Sunday School Union. Periodic reports of missionaries of the Union. 485 vols. 1825–1908. ASSUL
Catholic Foreign Mission Society of America Archives (including correspondence from China of several hundred missionaries). MF

Christian Women's Board of Missions. *See* United Christian Missionary Society.

Disciples of Christ. Materials relating to the Disciples of Christ in China. CBL

Disciples of Christ. *See* United Christian Missionary Society.

Episcopal Church (Protestant Episcopal Church in the United States of America). China Mission letters and papers, Shanghai, Wuhu (including Anking), and Hankow. 4 large boxes and 3 large cartons. 1850–1917. Ch.HS

Foreign Christian Missionary Society. *See* United Christian Missionary Society.

General Conference on Foreign Missions. Minute book, 1878 and 1888, and related materials. MRL

International Missionary Council (New York). Archives. Materials relating to China in several filing drawers. 1920's through 1940's. MRL

Laymen's Missionary Inquiry. Original papers, China and India. Several boxes and file drawers. 1931–1932. MRL

Maryknoll Fathers. *See* Catholic Foreign Mission Society of America.

Methodist Episcopal Church. Archives of the Methodist Episcopal Mission (Northern Methodists) are in the library of the Division of World Missions, Board of Missions of the Methodist Church. Materials more than fifty years old are available on microfilm to be used at the Board's library. The original papers are in storage.

Only scanty files of missionary correspondence from China are preserved for the period 1847–1912. These are in microfilm rolls, Nos. 6–11:

No. 6 Letters of bishops (from White to Bashford)

No. 7 Missionary correspondence: Central China

No. 8 Central China; North China

No. 9 North China; West China

No. 10 West China; Foochow; Hinghwa

No. 11 Hinghwa

Some papers of the Woman's Foreign Mission Society are included in No. 7.

Available in the same library are manuscript minutes of missionary meetings in China, 1847–1900, about 5 vols. There are also 8 file drawers of "project files" — including mostly printed materials on Methodist schools, colleges, and hospitals in China. MC:DWM

Methodist Episcopal Church. The Action of the General Conference Concerning Missions from 1792–1909. 175 pp., typewritten, MRL

Nanking Union Church. Records. 13 vols. 1916–1940. VUL

National Christian Council (Shanghai). Minutes. Looseleaf binders. 1922–1949. Compiled by Charles L. Boynton. MRL

National Christian Council (Shanghai). Papers. 17 looseleaf binders, mainly mimeographed material, covering a period up to 1950's. MRL

Presbyterian Church. Records of Presbyterian organizations in China, and papers concerning early missionary activities there. PRC:HF

Presbyterian Church. Presbyterian Foreign Mission Archives. China, 1837–1910. Available on microfilm. Detailed calendar, with a summary of each document, in 131 vols. (Note the duplication of volume numbers 41–58 and the absence of numbers 82–99.)

LETTERS, *1837–1910*, VOLS. *1–45*

1. 1837–1844 (Canton and Macao)
2. 1845–1846 (Macao, Amoy, and Ningpo)
3–4. 1845–1864 (Ningpo)
5. 1850–1864 (Shanghai)
6. 1845–1864 (Canton and Amoy)
7–20. 1862–1886 (All China)
21. 1887 (Canton)
22. 1887–1888 (All China)
23. 1888–1889 (North China)
24. 1889–1890 (Shantung and Peking)
25. 1890–1892 (Central China)
26. 1891–1892 (Shantung)
27. 1893–1894 (Shantung)
28. 1893–1894 (Canton)
29. 1893–1894 (Central China)
30. 1890–1894 (North China and Peking)
31. 1891–1895 (Hainan)
32. 1895–1896 (Canton)
33. 1895–1896 (North China and Peking)
34. 1895–1896 (Central China)
35. 1895–1896 (Shantung)
36. 1896–1898 (Hainan)
37. 1897–1898 (Central China)
38. 1897–1898 (South China and Canton)
39. 1899 (Central China)
40. 1897 (North China)
41. 1897–1900 (East Shantung)
42. 1899–1900 (Canton)
43. 1899–1900 (Hainan)
44. 1900 (Central China)
45. 1897–1900 (West Shantung)

MINUTES AND REPORTS, 1876–1900, VOLS. 46–58

46. Minutes, 1887–1900 (Central China)
47. Reports, 1888–1900 (Central China)
48. Minutes, 1896–1900 (Hainan)
49. Reports, 1893–1900 (Hainan)
50. Minutes, 1895–1900 (South China and Canton)
51. Reports, 1891–1900 (South China and Canton)
52. Reports, 1884–1886 (North China)
53. Minutes and Reports, 1876–1896 (Shantung)
54. Minutes, 1895–1900 (East Shantung)
55. Reports, 1895–1900 (East Shantung)
56. Minutes, 1895–1900 (West Shantung)
57. Reports, 1895–1900 (West Shantung)
58. Minutes and Reports, 1888–1900 (North China and Peking)

SOUTH CHINA AND CANTON, 1900–1910, VOLS. 41–54

41–51. Letters, 1900–1910
52. Outgoing letters, 1902–1906, 1911
53. Minutes, 1901–1910
54. Reports, 1901–1910

CENTRAL CHINA, 1900–1911, VOLS. 55–67

55–65. Letters, 1900–1910
66. Outgoing letters, 1900–1911
67. Personal reports, 1901–1910
(Station minutes and reports are bound and in the Library.)

HAINAN, 1900–1910, VOLS. 68–81

68–78. Letters, 1900–1910
79. Outgoing letters, 1894–1899, 1903–1911

80. Minutes, 1901–1910
81. Reports, 1901–1910

NORTH CHINA AND PEKING, 1901–1911, VOLS. 100–112

100–109. Letters, 1901–1910
110. Outgoing letters, 1901–1911
111. Minutes, 1901–1910
112. Reports, 1901–1910

SHANTUNG, 1901–1910, VOLS. 113–131

113–115. Letters, East Shantung, 1901–1903
116–118. Letters, West Shantung, 1901–1903
119–125. Letters, all Shantung, 1904–1910
126. Outgoing letters, East Shantung, 1902–1905, and all Shantung and East Shantung, 1909–1910
127. Outgoing letters, West Shantung, 1910–1911
128. Minutes, East Shantung, 1901–1910
129. Reports, East Shantung, 1901–1910
130. Minutes, West Shantung, 1901–1910
131. Reports, West Shantung, 1901–1910

Materials up to 1920 are being made available. PBFM, Pr. HS, and HC:WL

Reformed Church in America. Manuscript letters between the Board of Missions and the Amoy Mission. 1856–1900. NBTSL

Southern Baptist Convention, The Foreign Mission Board. Archives of missionary correspondence. SBC:-FMB

Student Volunteer Movement. Correspondence and records. 142 file drawers. 1888–1914. YU:DL

United Christian Missionary Society. Historical records of the various missions now merged into United Christian Missionary Society, including American Christian

Missionary Society, Christian Women's Board of Missions, and Foreign Christian Missionary Society. DHS

World's Student Christian Federation. Papers. 84 shelves, including published materials as well as manuscripts. YU:DL

Yale Missionary Society. Documents, including records of meetings. 1852–1865. YU:SL

YMCA. Chinese work in France: material on the Chinese Labor-Student Movement in France at the end of the First World War, 1 box. David Z. T. Yui Correspondence, 1 box, 1920–1921. YMCA:HL

YMCA. File of typed index cards on research materials concerning the YMCA in China. Compiled by C. Howard Hopkins and assistants. About 400 cards. YMCA:HL

YMCA. International Committee Archives. Among these extensive archives are at least 52 boxes containing correspondence received by the International Committee from YMCA secretaries and other personnel in China;

Boxes 22–28 contain letters specially selected from the archives for their value from the viewpoint of YMCA history, covering various Chinese cities, 1891–1950.

Boxes 59–105 cover the period 1891–1945. These are the original files, minus the materials now in Boxes 22–28.

Box 103. "Chungking Residences."

Box 104. Clifford W. Petitt's History of the YMCA in China.

Among the miscellaneous manuscripts at the Historical Library are the following:

Reports from various cities mostly in the 1920's. 6 boxes.

Shanghai Reports. 6 boxes. 1920's and 1930's. YMCA:HL

YMCA. National Committee, Student Division. Papers. At least 5 drawers. YU:DL

1.5 CHRISTIAN COLLEGES AND HOSPITALS

Anglo-Chinese College, Malacca. Papers. 1 box. 1825. MRL

China Medical Board of New York, Inc. Archives of the Board and materials on the Peking Union Medical College. CMBNY

Fagley, F. L., comp. Conspectus of American Contributions and Altruistic Interests in the Far East. YU:DL

Fukien Christian University. Papers. ABCFM Papers, ABC 16.3.14; HU:HL

Fukien Christian University. *See* United Board.

Ginling College. *See* United Board.

Hangchow University. *See* United Board.

Hua Chung College. Miscellaneous materials. NCPEC

Hua Chung College. *See* United Board.

Hwa Nan College. *See* United Board.

Lingnan University, Board of Trustees. Complete archives in 219 ream-size boxes. Mimeographed guide and index, 35 pp. The archives are in two main divisions:

Reports, minutes, and other documents, 1884–1951; including "Students and Alumni, 1915–46," and numerous student publications.

Correspondence, 1884–1951. HU:CJL

Microfilm in 43 rolls may be used at the United Board for Christian Higher Education in Asia, New York.

Nanking University. *See* United Board.

North China American School. Papers. ABCFM Papers, ABC 16.3.14; HU:HL

North China College. Papers. ABCFM Papers, ABC 16.3.14; HU:HL

North [China] and Union Colleges. Papers. ABCFM Papers, ABC 16.3.14; HU:HL

Peking Union Medical College. *See* China Medical Board of New York.

Princeton in Asia. Records, including reports and other materials of Princeton-in-Peking and Princeton–Yenching Foundation. 16 file drawers. 1920–1962. PIA

St. John's University. Miscellaneous materials. NCPEC

Shantung Christian University (Cheeloo). *See* United Board.

Soochow University. *See* United Board.

United Board for Christian Higher Education in Asia. The archives of the Board are in 156 boxes (letter-size, each containing about 1 ream), and are reproduced in 112 rolls of microfilm. Materials include reports, minutes, letters from persons in China or in the United States, college publications, student and alumni records. Typed indexes, 2 vols., available at the Board. Materials concerning individual institutions:

Fukien Christian University (8 microfilm rolls). Reports, minutes, and other documents, 1917–1951. Correspondence, 1920–1945.

Ginling College (8 rolls). Reports, minutes, and other documents, 1915–1948, including "Alumnae Directories, Statistics, & Biographical Notes" and "Ginling Rural Work." Correspondence, 1914–1948.

Hangchow University (formerly Hangchow Christian College, 4 rolls). Reports, minutes, and other documents, mostly dated 1930's and 1940's, including

"Alumni questionnaire." Correspondence, a few items, 1938–1945.

Hua Chung College (1 roll). Reports, minutes and other documents, 1928–1951, including "Yale-in-China, Bulletins and Reports, 1923–1950." Correspondence, 1923–1950.

Hwa Nan College (1 roll). Reports, minutes, and other documents, 1936–1949. Correspondence, 1933–1946.

University of Nanking (17 rolls). Reports, minutes, and other documents, mostly 1887–1945. Correspondence, 1910–1945.

Shantung Christian University (Cheeloo, 10 rolls). Reports, minutes, and other documents, mostly 1915–1951, including "Rural Program in Shantung," "Student Rebellion in Arts College, June 12–13, 1915," "Cheeloo and Revolution, 1925–30." Correspondence, 1915–1950.

Soochow University (1 roll). Reports, minutes, and other documents, mostly for the 1930's and 1940's. Correspondence, 1927–1945.

West China Union University (8 rolls). Reports, minutes, and other documents, 1910–1950, including "Political Situation in China, 1926–1927." Correspondence, 1916–1947.

Yenching University (originally Peking University, 24 rolls). Reports, minutes, and other documents, 1890–1950, including "Directories of Faculty and Students, 1923–1942," and Howard S. Galt, "Yenching University, Its Sources and Its History." Correspondence, 1918–1948.

Materials of the Associated Boards and the United Board (16 rolls):

Associated Boards for Christian Colleges in China.

Reports, minutes, and other documents, 1925–1950, including minutes of the Supervisory Committee for the Central Office of the China Union Universities, the Permanent Committee for the Coordination and Promotion of Christian Higher Education in China, 1925–1928, and the Committee for Christian Colleges in China, 1928–1932. Correspondence, 1918–1945. Accounting Records, 1923–1947.

United Board for Christian Colleges in China. Reports, minutes, and other documents, 1945–1948, including documents of the Associated Boards for Christian Colleges in China before 1945, and "Minutes of the Council of Higher Education, 1924–45." Accounting records, 1945–   . Postwar planning papers, 1944–1946, including Charles H. Corbett, "Christian Middle Schools in China under Protestant Auspices and Their Relation to the Christian Colleges" and Paul C. T. Kwei, "Reflections on Christian Colleges in China — an Outline." UBCHEA

West China Union University. *See* United Board.

Yale-in-China. Correspondence. 1901–1903. Carbon copies of early papers; also letters by A. C. Williams, A. P. Stokes, F. K. Sanders, J. L. Thurston, W. Sloane, H. P. Beach, J. C. Hollister, and twelve others. YU:SL

Yale-in-China. Early manuscripts. 4 cases. YU:SL

Yale-in-China. Miscellaneous letters of Henry Robinson Luce, Donald Cole McCabe, *et al.,* YU:SL

Yale-in-China. Papers. 2 file drawers. (The main body of the Yale-in-China material is to be found at the Sterling Library.) YU:DL

Yale-in-China. Papers collected by Lewis Sheldon Welch. 7 boxes. YU:SL

Yale-in-China. Papers of Henry W. Farnam on Yale affairs, Box A. YU:SL

Yale-in-China, Changsha, China. Correspondence and other documents. Collected by Henry P. Wright. 2 folders. YU:SL

Yenching-Peking Christian Colleges. Papers. 1889–1927. ABCFM Papers, ABC 16.3.14; HU:HL

Yenching (Peking) University. *See* United Board.

1.6 MISCELLANEOUS NONGOVERNMENTAL INSTITUTIONS IN THE UNITED STATES

American Asiatic Association. Minute-book. 1898–1900. *See* Charles S. Campbell, *Special Business Interests and the Open Door Policy* (New Haven, 1951).

American Committee for Nonparticipation in Japanese Aggression. Correspondence. 12 file drawers. 1938–1941. HU:LC

American National Red Cross. Archives, including correspondence and reports on relief work in China. 1881–1956. Open to research, subject to permission. ARC

League of Women Voters. Records. 966 boxes and 28 bundles. 1920–1950. LC

League of Women Voters of California. Papers. 12,000 pieces. 1922–1955. CHS

1.7 TRAVELERS AND JOURNALISTS

Anonymous passenger. Journal of the voyage of the *St. James* (bark), Capt. Tapley, master, New York to Hongkong and Norfolk. 1898–1899. MM

Crow, Carl. Papers. 3 vols. and 332 folders. 1903–1945. Mo.U

Embree, Edwin Rogers. Family journal. 1918–1934. YU:-SL

Kennan, George. Papers. 100 boxes, including manuscripts relating to Russia, Japan, and China. 1867–1937. LC

Low, Harriet. Journal (Macao). 2 boxes. 1829–1834. Low Family Papers; LC

McCormick, Frederick. Letters from China. Included in McCormick family papers, 10 feet, 1900–1941. Collection of Regional History; Cor.U

Morse, Richard Cary. Journal extracts. 1854–1855. YU:SL

Morse, Sidney Edwards. Journal of a Voyage to China on the *N. B. Palmer*. 1 vol. Aug. 2, 1856–April 12, 1857. YU:SL

Sokolsky, George Ephraim. Memoir. 45 pp., typewritten. 1956. Oral History Collection; CUL:SC

Tenney, P. G. Account of an expedition to Central China, 1923–1924. 1 vol. 1924. HU:HL

Wood, William W. Papers. 1 box. Mostly 1830's. HU:HL

Wulsin, Frederick R. Papers. 12 boxes, including materials on an expedition to Central China, 1923–1924. HU:HL

1.8 SCHOLARS AND ACADEMIC ORGANIZATIONS

American Council of Learned Societies. Records of the Joint Committee on Materials for Research of the American Council of Learned Societies and the Social Science Research Council. 18 cases. 1930–1939. LC

Bradley, Charles William. Letter sent from China in 1858 and notes on China. YU:SL

Brill, Gerow D. Papers. Correspondence and miscellaneous papers, including letters and account books of Brill when he was head of the Hupeh Agricultural College and Experimental Farm in Wuchang, around 1899. 1891–1917. Collection of Regional History; Cor.U

Cornell-in-China. *See* George J. Thompson.

Eliot, Charles William. Letters written during a trip to the Far East. 2 boxes. 1911–1912. The Eliot Papers; HU:WL

Griffin, Eldon. Working copy of his *Clippers and Consuls* (Ann Arbor, 1938), with additional material. 4 vols. HU:BL

Griffis, William Elliot. Papers. 120 boxes (including 4 on China). 1870–1927. RUL

Hance, Henry Fletcher. Materials chiefly concerning his botanical studies in China. 30 pieces. 1858–1882, HU:-AAGH

Harvard Medical School of China (Shanghai). Archives. Reports. 1 vol. 1911–1917. Financial records. 3 vols. 1910–1926. Also other materials. HU:SMPHL

Institute of Pacific Relations. Office files. 68 vols. and 118 file drawers. 1927–1957. CUL:SC

Institute of Pacific Relations. Records. 12 feet. 1925–1939. SU

Latourette, Kenneth Scott. Papers. YU:DL and YU:SL

Needham, James George. Papers, including journal of his trip to China. 2 feet. 1892–1956. Cor.U

Sheldon, Sidney R. Sheldon-Fife papers. 3 feet. 1818–1930. OUL

Stephens, Henry Morse. Papers. 1894–1922. University Archives; Cor.U

Thompson, George J., collector. Cornell-in-China Papers, including correspondence, particularly regarding Emergency Student Relief Program. 42 packages. 1935–1949. Cor.U

Williams, Frederick Wells. Papers. Included in the Williams family papers, a total of 28 boxes, 1774–1938. YU:SL

1.9 DIPLOMATS AND STATESMEN: PRIVATE PAPERS

For a full list of the papers of presidents and cabinet officers, see Hamer, *A Guide to Archives and Manuscripts in the United States.*

Allen, Horace N. Papers. 44 vols. and 300 pieces. 1884–1905. NYPL

Anderson, Chandler P. Papers. 101 boxes. 1914–1929. LC

Angell, James B. Papers, including materials on his mission to Peking. 51 boxes. 1866–1916. Mich.U

Auchincloss, Gordon. Papers. Edward M. House Collection; YU:SL

Avery, Benjamin Parke. Memoranda of Interviews with Li-Hung-Chang, 1874. UCB:GL

Baker, Ray Stannard. Papers, including 78 boxes of documents relating to his biography of Woodrow Wilson. 208 boxes. 1875–1948. LC

Borah, William E. Papers. 37 vols. and 718 boxes. 1912–1940. LC

Bryan, William Jennings. Papers. 16 vols., 88 boxes, and 5 portfolios. 1877–1931. LC

Burlingame family. Papers, including papers of Anson Burlingame and his son Edward Livermore Burlingame. 5 boxes. 1810–1922. LC

Burlingame family. 260 letters written from China and Europe by the sons of Anson Burlingame. 1851–1922. Syr.U

Chilton, Robert S. Papers, including letters of Hubbard T. Smith, consul in Canton. 237 items. 1808–1901. DUL

Cleveland, Grover. Papers. 407 vols. and 109 boxes. 1859–1910. LC

Colby, Bainbridge. Papers. 2500 items. 1887–1950. LC

Coolidge, Calvin. Papers. 347 boxes. 1923–1929. LC

Cushing, Caleb. Papers. 49 vols., 530 boxes, and 30 bundles. 1817–1879. LC

Cushing, Caleb. Papers. 1 envelope. 1829–1864. EI

Daniels, Josephus. Papers. 66 vols. and 960 boxes. 1813–1948. LC

Davis, Norman H. Papers. 93 boxes. 1918–1942. LC

Everett, Alexander Hill. Papers. 13 vols. and 3 boxes. 1818–1857. MHS

Foster, John Watson. Papers. 1 box. 1872–1917. LC

Foulk, George C. Papers. Approximately 1000 items, 1884–1887. NYPL

German legation, Peking. Materials from the archives. 580 items. 1868–1904. Trin.CL

Grant, Ulysses S. Papers. 95 vols., 6 boxes, and 3 packages. 1834–1885. LC

Gresham, Walter Q. Papers. 44 vols., 5 boxes, and 1 portfolio. 1857–1896. LC

Grew, Joseph C. Papers. 174 vols. and 30 folders. 1909–1945. HU:HL

Harding, Warren G. Papers. 4 boxes. 1897–1923. LC

Harrison, Leland. Papers. 123 boxes. 1915–1947. LC

Hay, John M. Papers. 15 vols. and 110 boxes. 1859–1914. LC

Hoover, Herbert. Extensive archives. Not open as of 1961. SU

Hopkins, Harry L. Papers. 125 cu. ft. 1928–1946. FDRL

House, Edward M. Papers. 92 file drawers and 94 boxes. 1880–1926. YU:SL

Hughes, Charles Evans. Papers. 57 vols., 16 boxes, 4 packing cases, and 8 filing drawers. LC

Hull, Cordell. Papers. 33,000 pieces. 1910–1950. LC

Huntington-Wilson, Francis M. Papers. Urs.CL

Huston, Jay C. Papers. 18 boxes. 1917–1931. Hoover Institution on War, Revolution, and Peace; SU

Johnson, Nelson T. Memoir. 730 pp., typewritten. 1954. Oral History Collection; CUL:SC

Johnson, Nelson T. Papers. 45 vols. and 2 boxes. 1916–1950. LC

Kellogg, Frank B. Papers. 21 vols. and 33 boxes. 1907–1937. Minn.HS

Knox, Philander C. Papers. 27 vols. and 5 boxes. 1796–1922. LC

Lansing, Robert. Papers. 62 vols. and 3 boxes. 1911–1928. LC

LeGendre, Charles William (consul at Amoy, China). 23 vols. and 11 boxes. 1868–1892. LC

Lodge, Henry Cabot. Papers. 120 boxes. 1745–1924. MHS

Long, Breckinridge. Papers (including diplomatic reports, 1917–1920). 130 vols. and 86 boxes. 1775–1944. LC

McKinley, William. Papers. 261 vols. and 156 boxes. 1847–1902. LC

Marshall, George C. A large quantity of the general's papers, not available to scholars as of 1962. MRC

Moffat, Jay Pierrepont. Papers. 44 vols. and 5 boxes. HU:HL

Morgenthau, Henry, Jr. Papers. 300 cu. ft. 1866–1948. FDRL

Olney, Richard. Papers. 153 vols., 15 boxes, and 3 bundles. 1830–1917. LC

Phillips, William. Memoir. 165 pp., typewritten. 1951. Oral History Collection; CUL:SC

Pittman, Key. Papers. LC

Pittman, Key. Papers. 1904–1933. NHS

Polk, Frank L. Papers. Edward M. House Collection; YU:SL

Reed, William B. Papers. 1 vol. and 1 piece. 1857–1859. LC

Roberts, Edmund. Papers. 10 vols and 5 boxes. 1805–1836. LC

Roberts, Edmund. Papers. 1 box. 1815–1836. NHHS

Rockhill, William W. Papers. 3000 pieces. 1874–1914. HU:HL

Roosevelt, Franklin D. Papers, including papers of Mr. Roosevelt as president, 1933–1945. FDRL

Roosevelt, Theodore. Papers. 266 vols., 904 boxes, and 15 envelopes. 1870–1940. LC

Root, Elihu. Papers. 73 vols. and 312 boxes. 1898–1937. LC

Rosenman, Samuel I. Papers. 21 cu. ft. 1928–1946. FDRL

Schurman, Jacob Gould. Papers. 45 boxes. 1878–1942. Cor.U

Seward, George Frederick. Papers. 4 boxes. 1890–1910. NYHS

Sherman, John. Papers. 613 vols. and 12 boxes. 1846–1894. LC

Stettinius, Edward R. Papers. 750,000 pieces. 1914–1949. VUL

Stimson, Henry L. Papers. 50,000 items, 1892–1950, including his diary, 1910–1945. Historical Manuscripts Collection; YU:SL

Straight, Willard. Papers. 90 feet of material. 1857–1922. Cor.U

Taft, William Howard. Papers. 1300 boxes. 1810–1921. LC

Truman, Harry S. Papers, including papers of Mr. Truman as president, 1945–1953. HSTL

Viner, Jacob. Memoir. 61 pp., typewritten. 1953. Oral History Collection; CUL:SC

Wallace, Henry A. Papers. 37 cu. ft. 1941–1945. FDRL

Wallace, Henry A. Papers. 9 scrapbooks, 11 cartons, and 4 transfer cases. 1941–1944. LC

Williams, Samuel Wells. Papers. Included in the Williams family papers, a total of 28 boxes, 1774–1938. YU:SL

Wilson, Woodrow. Papers. 1322 boxes. 1880–1924. LC

Young, John Russell. Papers. 34 vols. and 3 boxes. 1854–1898. LC

1.10   MILITARY MEN: PRIVATE PAPERS

Beardslee, Lester A., Acting Master, U.S. sloop of war *Germantown*. Diary–Norfolk to Cape Town, Hongkong, Nagasaki, etc. 1857–1860. MM

Beardslee, Lt. Commander Lester A., U.S. gunboat *Aroostook*. Diary and letterbook–Cruising, Amoy, Loochoo, Formosa, etc. 1868. MM

Bliss, Tasker H. Papers. 1870–1937. LC

Bonaparte, Charles J. Papers. 1874–1921. LC

Bristol, Mark L. 1887–1928. 162 boxes. LC

Corbin, Henry Clark. Papers. 18 vols. and 9 boxes, including materials on the Boxer Rebellion. 1865–1905. LC

Dewey, George. Papers. 1880–1917. LC

Kearny, Lawrence. Papers. 5 vols. of logbooks and letterbooks. 1814–1844. NJHS

Knox, William Franklin. Papers. 1898–1944. LC

Leahy, William D. Diaries. 15 vols. 1897–1952. LC

Long, John D. Papers. 1863–1922. MHS

McCoy, Frank R. Papers. 1847–1949. 95 boxes. LC

Meyer, George von Lengerke. Papers. 1900–1918. MHS

Moody, William H. Papers. 1879–1916. LC

Remey, George C. Papers. 1855–1930. LC

Shufeldt, Robert W. Papers. 22 boxes. 1864–1884. LC

Stilwell, Joseph W. Papers, including diaries. 18 vols. and 10 boxes. 1941–1944. Hoover Institution on War, Revolution and Peace; SU

Yarnell, Harry Ervin. Papers. 11 boxes. 1936–1939. LC

1.11 UNITED STATES GOVERNMENT ARCHIVES

For the extensive records in the National Archives, the following guides should be consulted:

General

    Guide to the Records in the National Archives. Washington, 1948; 684 pp.

Diplomatic

    Eckhoff, Mark G., and Alexander P. Mavro. *List of Foreign Service Post Records in the National Archives.* Special List No. 9. Rev. ed. Washington, 1958; 48 pp.

    Helton, H. Stephen. *Records of the United States Participation in International Conferences, Commissions, and Expositions.* Preliminary Inventory No. 76. Washington, 1955; 161 pp.

    Maddox, John E. *Records of the American War Production Mission in China.* Preliminary Inventory No. 88. Washington, 1955; 10 pp.

    Mavro, Alexander P. *Records of Selected Foreign Service Posts.* Preliminary Inventory No. 60. Washington, 1953; 51 pp.

    Spielman, Herbert. "The Accessibility of Department of State Materials Relating to American Far Eastern Relations," *Far Eastern Quarterly,* 15:97–103 (1955–1956).

    Summers, Natalia. *List of Documents Relating to Special Agents of the Department of State, 1789–1906.* Special List No. 7. Washington, 1951; 229 pp.

Military

    Federal Records of World War II. Washington, 1950, 1951; 2 vols. (Vol. II deals exclusively with military agencies; it contains descriptions of the records and their location.)

    Huber, Elbert L. "War Department Records in the National Archives," *Military Affairs,* 6:247–254 (1942).

    Morton, Louis. "Sources for the History of World War II," *World Politics,* 13:435–453 (1961).

    Pendell, Lucille H., and Elizabeth Bethel. *Records of the Adjutant General's Office.* Preliminary Inventory No. 17. Washington, 1949; 149 pp.

    Nearly 500 rolls of microfilm pertaining to the diplomatic, consular, and naval relations between the United States and Far Eastern countries from the late eighteenth century until 1906 are available on the West Coast at the universities of Washington and Southern California; in the Midwest at the universities of Indiana and Wisconsin; and in the

South at the University of Florida. Individual rolls of positives may be ordered directly 'from the National Archives at a nominal cost. See *List of National Archives Microfilm Publications 1961*. Washington, 1961; 231 pp.

Microfilm or photostats of other parts of the archives accessible to research may also be ordered through the National Archives. Negatives for these reproductions have to be specially made for each order.

The student may also gain access to the Federal Records Centers administered by the Office of Records Management of the General Services Administration. These depositories contain for the most part noncurrent and semicurrent field records of government agencies. Sixteen depositories are outside of the Washington area: Chicago; Clearfield, Utah; Denver; Dorchester, Mass.; East Point, Ga.; Fort Worth; Honolulu; Kansas City, Mo.; Mechanicsburg, Pa.; New Orleans; New York; Philadelphia; St. Louis; Seattle; South San Francisco; and Wilmington, Calif. A seventeenth is at Alexandria, Va.; this administers semicurrent records of government branches at Washington, D.C., and has the best collection of World War II records. The researcher's use of these depositories requires permission. For details, see Philip M. Hamer, *A Guide to Archives and Manuscripts in the United States* (New Haven, 1961).

Adjutant General's Office. Records. Record Group 94; US:NA

Agriculture, Department of. General Records. Record Group 16; US:NA

American Expeditionary Forces, 1917–1921. Records. Record Group 120; US:NA

Army Air Forces. Records. Record Group 18; US:NA and US:AF

Commerce, Department of. General Records. Record Group 40; US:NA

Foreign Economic Administration. Records. Record Group 169; US:NA (See H. Stephen Helton, *Records of the Foreign Economic Administration,* Preliminary Inventory No. 29. Washington, 1951; 180 pp.)

Marine Corps, United States. Records. Record Group 127; US:NA

Navy, Department of. Records of the Office of the Chief of Naval Operations. Record Group 38; US:NA

Navy, Department of. Records of the Office of the Chief of Naval Operations. Historical materials including operation plans, war diaries, battle reports, and other naval records for the period during and after World War II. US:ND

Navy, Department of. General Records. Record Group 80; US:NA (Some divisions of the Navy Department archives before 1906 are available on microfilm. See *List of National Archives Microfilm Publications 1961*.)

Office of War Information. Records. Record Group 208; US:NA (See H. Stephen Helton, *Records of the Office of War Information*, Preliminary Inventory No. 56. Washington, 1953; 149.)

Presidential Committees, Commissions, and Boards. Records. Record Group 220; US:NA

State, Department of. Records. With the exception of a few categories of passport, visa, unsettled claims, and personal debts, the records of the Department of State for the period up to Jan. 1, 1930, are completely open. As of 1962, materials for the period 1930–1942 are only available under certain conditions to more mature and qualified researchers, including Ph.D. candidates. Permission to use these materials must be obtained through the Chief of the Historical Division, Department of State, Washington, D.C. The Department of State materials in the National Archives fall into three general "record groups." These are:

General Records of the Department of State, Record Group 59; US:NA

Records of the Foreign Service Posts of the Department of State, Record Group 84; US:NA

United States Participation in International Conferences, Commissions, and Expositions, Record Group 43; US:NA

War Department. Records of the General Staff. Record Group 165; US:NA

War Department. Records of the Office of the Secretary of War. Record Group 107; US:NA (Some divisions of the War Department archives before 1906 are available on microfilm. See *List of National Archives Microfilm Publications 1961.*)

1.12 AMERICANS IN THE SERVICE OF THE CHINESE GOVERNMENT

Baker, John Earl. Fighting China's Famine. 476 pp., typewritten. 1943. MRL

Drew, Edward B. The Present Condition of China. Manuscript for a Lowell Institute lecture. 80 pp. 1881–1882. HU:HL

Goodnow, Frank J. Papers. 14,600 items. 1891–1932. JHU

Merrill, H. F. Letters to Sir Robert Hart and others in the Chinese Customs Service. Typed transcripts. 2 boxes. 1884–1913. HU:HL

Morse, Hosea Ballou. Letterbooks of semiofficial correspondence while serving as Commissioner of Chinese maritime customs. Press copies and manuscript copies. 5 vols. 1886–1907. Also typewritten transcripts. HU:HL Note Morse's collection of Sir Robert Hart's papers: Letters to various Westerners in the Chinese customs service, typewritten transcripts, 1 box, 1865–1910; and Papers concerning Chinese Inspectorate General of Customs, originals and typewritten transcripts, 1 box, 1885–1909, including letters to E. B. Drew and H. B. Morse. HU:HL

1.13 CHINESE IN THE UNITED STATES

American Missionary Association. Archives. About 48 chests, including materials on the Chinese mission in San Francisco. 1839–1879. FUL

Bagley, Clarence Booth. Papers on Pacific Northwest history; contain materials on anti-Chinese riot in Seattle, 1866. 750 items. 1841–1916. WUL

Bancroft, Hubert Howe. Reference notes on California (containing materials on the Chinese), 4 vols., 1769–1886. Clippings on the Chinese, 1850–1890. UCB:BL

"Bill" (San Francisco), Letter to "Nell," July 12, 1854. Describes Chinese bathhouse. YU:SL

Cary, Thomas Greaves. The Chinese in California. 1 vol., typewritten. 60 pp. YU:SL and BA

Chinese Business Records. Nevada County, California, 4 cartons and 1 box (mainly Chinese manuscripts), 1870–1912. Placer County, California, 2 portfolios, 1884–1915. UCB:BL

Chinese Students' Alliance of Hawaii. Records. 3 vols. 1906–1911. UCB:BL

Cleveland, Daniel. Letters concerning Chinese in California. 4 items. 1868–1872. UCB:BL

Disciples of Christ, Woman's Missionary Society, California North. Minutes of Meetings (including materials on the Chinese Christian Institute, San Francisco). 2 vols. Jan. 1914-Jan. 1937. UCB:BL

Haller, Granville Owen. A brief account of the anti-Chinese riot in Seattle, Feb. 7, 1886, written on the back of a photograph. YU:SL

Hartwell, J. B. Correspondence, including materials on the Baptist mission to the Chinese in California. 1857–1910. SBC:FMB

Huntington, Charles Andrew. Memoirs. Containing materials on the expulsion of Chinese from Eureka and Humboldt County, California. 224 pp., typewritten. 1899. YU:SL

Huntington, Collis Potter. Papers, consisting of correspondence with his partner, Mark Hopkins, relating to the Central Pacific, Western Pacific, and Southern Pacific Railroads. 14 vols. 1863–1887. SU

Labor agreements. Agreement (in English and Chinese) signed by Ti Kiet, Cantonese laborer, to work for the Panama Railroad Company, William O. Comstock, attorney. Feb. 20, 1854. NYHS

Labor agreements and indentures, including those of Chinese workers in California. HU:BL

Lee Foot Goong. Papers. 3 folders (mainly in Chinese). 1906–1933. UCB:BL

Loomis, Augustus Ward. Articles and letters on Chinese in California. 5 folders. 1876. UCB:BL

Loomis, Augustus Ward. Letters. In volume of letters relating to the Presbyterian Mission to the San Francisco Chinese. Pr.HS

Manion, John J. Chinese Tongs, 39 pp. Chinatown, 28 pp. UCB:BL

Miscellaneous records of missionary work among Chinese and Japanese in California. PSRL

Robinet, W. M. and G. M. 1 letterbook (in Spanish), containing materials on the coolie trade to the Americas. 1851–1853. Heard Papers; HU:BL

Simmons, E. J. Correspondence, including materials on the Baptist mission to the Chinese in California. 1869–1911. SBC:FMB

Speer, William. Letters. In volume of letters relating to

the Presbyterian Mission to the San Francisco Chinese. 1852–1865. Pr.HS

Tait & Co. (Amoy), letter to William O. Comstock, Nov. 3, 1853. NYHS

Young family. Papers (mainly in Chinese). 30 folders. 1924–1935. UCB:BL

1.14 "AMERICA-RETURNED" CHINESE

Among the biographical memoirs being produced in 1962 by the Oral History Project; East Asian Institute, Columbia University, were those of Ch'en Kuang-fu, Ch'en Li-fu, Hu Shih, Wellington V. K. Koo, J. Hung Liu, and Wang Cheng-t'ing. Typewritten copies of completed memoirs are deposited at the Special Collections Department of the Columbia University Libraries.

K'ung Hsiang-hsi. Reminiscences, as told to Julie Lien-Ying How, February 10 to June 10, 1958. 147 pp., typewritten. Chinese Oral History Project; CUL:SC

La Fargue, Thomas E. Manuscript materials relating to La Fargue's *China's First Hundred*. SCWL

Lew, Timothy Tingfang. Papers. Several cases of manuscripts, clippings, etc. MRL

Patterson, Lincoln E. Scrapbook, containing correspondence and other materials relating to Chinese students at Cornell. 3 vols. 1912–1937. Cor.U

Robinson, Arthur G. Collection of materials on the earliest Chinese students in the United States (the Yung Wing mission). HU:CJL

Twichell, Joseph H. Journals (containing letters by and information on Yung Wing). 12 vols. 1874–1912. YU:SL

Wu Kuo-cheng. Reminiscences for the years 1946–1953, recorded in April 1963. 391 pp., typewritten. Chinese Oral History Project; CUL:SC

Yen, Yang-ch'u, letter to Wilbur L. Cross, Aug. 24, 1928,

together with letters to or about Mr. Yen and biographical notes concerning him. YU:SL

Yui, David Z. T. *See* YMCA.

Yung, Bartlett Golden (Shanghai), letter to Jane Bartlett Kellogg, March 17, 1941. YU:SL

Yung Wing. 8 letters to Samuel Wells Williams, dated 1849–1878; Williams family papers. YU:SL

Yung Wing. 11 letters dated 1848 to 1910, to various persons. YU:SL

Yung Wing. 2 pieces in Chinese, with English translation. 1853–1854. YU:SL

2. BIOGRAPHIES, MEMOIRS, AND PUBLISHED LETTERS

2.1 Travelers and Sailors
 1784–1860
 1861–1900
 1901–1949
2.2 Merchants and Entrepreneurs
 Biographical collections
 1784–1900
 1901–1949
2.3 Missionaries
 Protestant missionaries
  Biographical collections: general
  Biographical collections: denominational
  1830–1900
  1901–1949
 Catholic missionaries
  Biographical collections
  Individual biographies
2.4 Doctors
 Biographical collections
 Individual biographies
2.5 Journalists
2.6 Scholars and Writers
 Biographical collections
 Individual biographies
2.7 Diplomats and Consuls
2.8 Military Men
2.9 Americans in the Service of the Chinese Government
2.10 Chinese Who Went to the United States
 Chinese in the United States
  Biographical collections
  Individual biographies
 "America-returned" Chinese
  Biographical collections
  Individual biographies

Section 2.1 contains a list of American travel literature concerned with China, the bulk of which is not covered by E. G. Cox's *A Reference Guide to the Literature of Travel* (Seattle, 1938). This section will serve to introduce the sections on Americans who resided in China or were otherwise professionally concerned with that country. Also included are the comparatively few English-language biographies and memoirs of Chinese laborers, merchants, and students in the United States.

"Memoirs" are defined in the narrow sense of personal records. Not included, therefore, are American writings on China in the following categories: studies of Chinese life; reporting of current events; and interpretations of China's problems. Works in these categories may be pursued in the bibliographies of Tung-li Yuan, Valentin H. Rabe, and Clayton H. Chu.

"Published letters" include only those that have appeared in book form or in journal articles. The reader will need to investigate government publications and periodical sources. For a selected list of mission magazines in the United States, which often reproduce extracts from letters of missionaries overseas, see section 3.1.

2.1   TRAVELERS AND SAILORS
1784–1860

[Anderson, John] Gale, Esson M. "Far Eastern Trade Routes and Cargoes: A New England Ship Captain's Letters, 1850–1856," Pacific Coast Branch, American Historical Association, *Proceedings*, 5:119–134 (1930).

[Appleton, Nathaniel] Phillips, James Duncan, ed. "Nathaniel Appleton's Journal of the Voyage of the Ship Concord Around the World, October 1799 to July 1802," Essex Institute, *Historical Collections*, 83:146–161, 220–246 (1947).

Ball, Benjamin Lincoln. *Rambles in Eastern Asia, Including China and Manila, during Several Years' Residence*. Boston, 1855; 471 pp.

[Barber, Henry] Howay, Frederic William. "Captain Henry Barber of Barber's Point," Hawaiian Historical Society, *Annual Report*, 47:39–49 (1939).

Blaney, Henry. *Journal of Voyage to China and Return, 1851–1853*. Boston, 1913; 134 pp.

Boit, John. "Boit's Log of the Columbia, 1790–1792," Massachusetts Historical Society, *Proceedings*, 53:217–275 (1919–1920).

Boit, John. "John Boit's Log of the Columbia — 1790–1793," Oregon Historical Society, *Quarterly*, 22:257–351 (1921).

[Collins, Perry McDonough] Swan, James G. "Explorations of the Amoor River: and its Importance on the Future Great Inter-Oceanic Trade Across the American Continent," *Hunt's Merchants' Magazine and Commercial Review*, 39:176–182 (1858).

[Colnett, James] Howay, Frederic William, ed. *The Journal of Captain James Colnett Aboard the Argonaut from April 26, 1789 to Nov. 3, 1791.* Toronto, 1940; 328 pp.

Delano, Amasa. *A Narrative of Voyages and Travels, in the Northern and Southern Hemispheres . . .* Boston, 1817; 598 pp.

Fanning, Edmund. *Voyages Round the World; with Selected Sketches of Voyages to the South Seas . . .* New York, 1833; 499 pp.

Gragg, William F. *A Cruise in the U.S. Steam Frigate Mississippi, Wm. C. Nicholson, Captain, to China and Japan, from July, 1857, to February, 1860.* Boston, 1860; 76 pp.

[Gray, Robert] Smith, Francis E. *Achievements and Experiences of Captain Robert Gray, 1788 to 1792,* 2nd ed. Tacoma, Wash., [1923]; 16 pp.

[Gray, Robert, and John Kendrick] Howay, Frederic William. "Captains Gray and Kendrick: The Barrell Letters," *Washington Historical Quarterly*, 12:243–271 (1921).

Habersham, Alexander Wylly. *My Last Cruise; or . . . Visits to the Malay and Loo-Choo Islands, the Coasts of China, Formosa, Japan . . .* Philadelphia, 1857; 507 pp.

[Holbrook, Silas Pinckney] *Sketches, by a Traveller.* Boston, 1830; 315 pp.

Howay, Frederic William, "Early Followers of Captain Gray," *Washington Historical Quarterly,* 18:11–20 (1927).

[Kendrick, John] Howay, Frederic William. "John Kendrick and His Sons," Oregon Historical Society, *Quarterly,* 23:277–302 (1922).

[Kendrick, John] Pipes, Nellie B. "Later Affairs of Kendrick; Barrell Letters," *Oregon Historical Quarterly,* 30:95–105 (1929).

Lawrence, James B. *China and Japan, and a Voyage Thither: An Account of a Cruise in the Waters of the East Indies, China, and Japan.* Hartford, 1870; 444 pp.

[Ledyard, John] Munford, Kenneth. *John Ledyard: An American Marco Polo.* Portland, Ore., 1939; 308 pp.

[Ledyard, John] Sparks, Jared. *The Life of John Ledyard, The American Traveller; Comprising Selections from His Journals and Correspondence.* Cambridge, Mass., 1828; 325 pp.

[Ledyard, John] [Sparks, Jared.] *Travels and Adventures of John Ledyard . . . ,* 2nd ed. London, 1834; 428 pp.

Little, George. *Life on the Ocean, or Twenty Years at Sea . . .* Baltimore, 1843; 395 pp.

[Low, Francis] Loines, Elma, ed. "Francis Low, A Salem Youth Dies on Board Ship in the China Sea," Essex Institute, *Historical Collections,* 87:261–268 (1951).

[Low, Harriet] Hillard, Katharine, ed. *My Mother's*

Journal; A Young Lady's Diary of Five Years Spent in Manila, Macao, and the Cape of Good Hope from 1829–1834. Boston, 1900; 320 pp.

[Low, Harriet] Hummel, Arthur W. "The Journal of Harriet Low," Library of Congress, *Quarterly Journal of Current Acquisitions,* 2.3 and 4:45–60 (1945).

[Metcalfe, Simon] Howay, Frederic William. "Captain Simon Metcalfe and the Brig 'Eleanora,'" *Washington Historical Quarterly,* 16:114–121 (1925).

Minturn, Robert B., Jr. *From New York to Delhi, By Way of Rio de Janeiro, Australia, and China.* London, 1858; 466 pp.

[Palmer, Nathaniel Brown] Spears, John R. *Captain Nathaniel Brown Palmer, an Old-Time Sailor of the Sea.* New York, 1922; 252 pp.

Shewan, Andrew. *The Great Days of Sail, Some Reminiscences of a Tea-Clipper Captain,* ed. Rex Clements. Boston, 1927; 240 pp.

Stewart, Charles Samuel. *A Visit to the South Seas, in the U. S. Ship Vincennes during the years 1829 and 1830* . . . New York, 1831; 2 vols.

Swisher, Earl. "The Adventure of Four Americans in Korea and Peking in 1855," *Pacific Historical Review,* 21:237–241 (1952).

Taylor, Bayard. *A Visit to India, China and Japan, in the Year 1853.* New York, 1855; 539 pp.

Taylor, Fitch W. *The Flag-ship: or, A Voyage Around the World in the United States Frigate Columbia.* New York, 1840; 2 vols.

[Tilden, Bryant Parrot] Jenkins, Lawrence Waters. *Bryant Parrot Tilden of Salem, at a Chinese Dinner Party, Canton: 1819.* [Princeton], 1944; 28 pp.

White, John. *History of a Voyage to the China Sea.* Boston, 1823; 372 pp.

1861–1900

Bainbridge, William F. *Around the World Tour of Christian Missions: A Universal Survey,* 2nd ed. Boston, 1882; 583 pp.

Ballou, Maturin M. *Due West; Or, Round the World in Ten Months.* Boston, 1884; 387 pp.

Bradford, Ruth. *"Maskee!" The Journal and Letters of Ruth Bradford, 1861–1872.* Hartford, 1938; 162 pp.

Brooks, James. *A Seven Months' Run, Up, and Down, and Around the World.* New York, 1872; 375 pp.

Brown, Charles W. *The Journal & Letters of Captain Charles W. Brown, 1876–1884.* [Cuyahoga Falls, Ohio], 1935; 110 pp.

[Burlingame, Jane Livermore] Walsh, Warren B., ed. "The Beginnings of the Burlingame Mission," *Far Eastern Quarterly,* 4:274–277 (1944–1945).

[Burlingame, Walter Anson] Walsh, Warren B., ed. "A Bandit Threat to the Burlingame Mission," *Far Eastern Quarterly,* 5:455–460 (1945–1946).

[Burlingame, Walter Anson] Walsh, Warren B., ed. "A Visit to the Tsungli Yamen," *Pacific Historical Review,* 14:452–454 (1945).

[Burlingame, Walter Anson] Walsh, Warren B., ed. "Young Yankee in China," *Pacific Historical Review,* 15:322–335 (1946).

Carnegie, Andrew. *Round the World.* New York, 1884; 360 pp.

Coffin, Charles Carleton. *Our New Way Round the World.* Boston, 1869; 524 pp.

Curtis, Benjamin Robbins. *Dottings Round the Circle.* Boston, 1876; 329 pp.

Davis, George. *Recollections of a Sea Wanderer's Life; An Autobiography of an Old-Time Seaman* . . . New York, 1887; 408 pp.

Farnham, John Marshall Willoughby. *Homeward; or, Travels in the Holy Land, China, India, Egypt, and Europe.* London, 1878; 307 pp.

Fogg, William Perry. *"Round the World." Letters from Japan, China, India and Egypt.* Cleveland, 1872; 237 pp.

Ford, John D. *An American Cruiser in the East; Travels and Studies in the Far East; the Aleutian Islands, Behring's Sea; Eastern Siberia, Japan, Korea, China, Formosa, Hong Kong, and the Philippine Islands.* New York, 1898; 468 pp.

[Grant, Ulysses S.] Young, John Russell. *Around the World with General Grant* . . . New York, [1879]; 2 vols.

Hart, Virgil C. *Western China; A Journey to the Great Buddhist Centre of Mount Omei.* Boston, 1888; 306 pp.

Hinckley, Frederic. *Wrecked on a Reef in the China Sea* . . . Boston, 1898; 20 pp.

Jones, W. P. "Description of a Voyage of Three Hundred and Fifty Miles up the Pearl or Canton River in China," American Geographical and Statistical Society, *Proceedings,* 2.4:93–109 (1864).

Kingsley, Calvin. *Round the World: A Series of Letters.* Vol. II. *Asia.* Cincinnati, 1871; 2 vols.

McLean, Archibald. *A Circuit of the Globe; A Series of Letters of Travel Across the American Continent, through the Hawaiian Republic, Japan, China, the*

Straits Settlements, Burma, India, Ceylon . . . St. Louis, 1897; 384 pp.

Miln, Louise Jordan. *When We Were Strolling Players in the East.* New York, 1894; 354 pp.

Moerlein, George. *A Trip Around the World.* Cincinnati, 1886; 205 pp.

Price, Julius M. *From the Arctic Ocean to the Yellow Sea. The Narrative of a Journey, in 1890 and 1891, across Siberia, Mongolia, the Gobi Desert, and North China.* London, 1892; 384 pp.

Pumpelly, Raphael. *Across America and Asia. Notes of a Five Years' Journey Around the World, and of Residence in Arizona, Japan, and China.* New York, 1870; 454 pp.

Rockhill, William Woodville. *Diary of a Journey through Mongolia and Thibet in 1891 and 1892.* Washington, 1894; 413 pp.

Rockhill, William Woodville. *The Land of the Lamas; Notes of a Journey through China, Mongolia and Tibet.* New York, 1891; 399 pp.

Seward, Olive Risley. *Around the World Stories,* Boston, 1889; 346 pp.

[Seward, William Henry] Seward, Olive Risley. *William H. Seward's Travels Around the World.* New York, 1873; 730 pp.

Sewell, John S. *The Logbook of the Captain's Clerk; Adventures in the China Seas.* Bangor, Me., 1905; 278 pp.

Simpson, Albert B. *Larger Outlooks on Missionary Lands, Descriptive Sketches of a Missionary Journey through Egypt, Palestine, India, Burmah, Malaysia, China, Japan and the Sandwich Islands.* New York, 1893; 595 pp.

Simpson, William. *Meeting the Sun: A Journey All Round the World, Through Egypt, China, Japan, and*

California, including an account of the marriage ceremonies of the Emperor of China. London, 1874; 413 pp.

Stern, Simon Adler. *Jottings of Travel in China and Japan.* Philadelphia, 1888; 185 pp.

Stevens, Thomas. *Around the World on a Bicycle.* New York, 1887–1888; 2 vols.

Taylor, Bayard. "Central Asia," American Geographical and Statistical Society of New York, *Proceedings,* 2.2:59–77 (1863–1864).

Williams, Martha [Noyes]. *A Year in China; and a Narrative of Capture and Imprisonment . . . on Board the Rebel Pirate Florida.* New York, 1864; 362 pp.

1901–1949

Bates, Lindon W., Jr. *The Russian Road to China.* Boston, 1910; 391 pp.

Brockway, Alice [Pickford]. *Letters from the Far East.* Philadelphia, 1919; 75 pp.

Cary, Melbert B. *The Estivation of Two Mao Tzu.* New York, 1935; 124 pp.

Close, Upton [Josef Washington Hall]. *In the Land of the Laughing Buddha; The Adventures of an American Barbarian in China.* New York, 1924; 359 pp.

Curtis, Claude H. *A Marine Among the Idols.* Grand Rapids, 1940; 79 pp.

Devins, John Bancroft. *On the Way to Hwai Yuen: Or, the Story of a Mule Ride in China Visiting the Presbyterian Mission in the An-Hui Province.* [New York], 1905; 90 pp.

Enders, Elizabeth Crump. *Swinging Lanterns.* New York, 1923, 358 pp.

Enders, Elizabeth Crump. *Temple Bells and Silver Sails.* New York, 1925; 337 pp.

Enders, Gordon B. *Foreign Devil; An American Kim in Modern Asia.* New York, 1942; 307 pp.

Erdman, Charles R. *Within the Gateways of the Far East; A Record of Recent Travel.* New York, 1922; 128 pp.

Forman, Harrison. *Horizon Hunter; The Adventures of a Modern Marco Polo.* New York, 1940; 314 pp.

Forman, Harrison. *Through Forbidden Tibet; An Adventure Into the Unknown.* New York, 1935; 275 pp.

Foster, Harry L. *A Beachcomber in the Orient.* New York, 1923; 395 pp.

Franck, Harry A. *Roving Through Southern China.* New York, 1925; 649 pp.

Franck, Harry A. *Wandering in Northern China.* New York, 1923; 502 pp.

Gardner, George Peabody, Jr. *Chiefly the Orient; An Undigested Journal* . . . [Norwood, Mass.], 1912; 378 pp.

Geil, William Edgar. *A Yankee on the Yangtze; Being a Narrative of a Journey from Shanghai through the Central Kingdom to Burma.* New York, 1904; 312 pp.

Headland, Isaac Taylor. *The Young China Hunters; A Trip to China by a Class of Juniors in 1912.* West Medford, Mass., 1912; 85 pp.

Kemp, Emily Georgiana. *The Face of China; Travels in . . . China; with Some Account of the New Schools, Universities, Missions, and the Old Religious Sacred Places* . . . London, 1909; 275 pp.

Kendall, Elizabeth K. *A Wayfarer in China; Impressions of a Trip Across West China and Mongolia.* Boston, 1913; 388 pp.

Lamont, Florence Haskell (Corliss). *Far Eastern Diary, 1920.* New York, 1951; 95 pp.

La Motte, Ellen N. *Peking Dust.* New York, 1919; 240 pp.

Longworth, Alice Roosevelt. *Crowded Hours; Reminiscences of Alice Roosevelt Longworth.* New York, 1933; 355 pp.

Mills, Annette T. *China Through a Car-Window: Observations on the Modern China, Made in the Course of a Four Months' Journey in Behalf of the Chinese Deaf; With Some Account of the School at Chefoo . . .* Washington, 1910; 53 pp.

Morse, Edward S. *Glimpses of China and Chinese Homes.* Boston, 1902; 216 pp.

Nichols, Francis H. *Through Hidden Shensi.* New York, 1902; 333 pp.

Nye, Jean Palmer. *Ricsha Rambles.* Boston, 1930; 238 pp.

Ortman, Blanche Sellers. *New York to Peking.* San Francisco, 1921; 146 pp.

Roosevelt, Theodore, and Kermit Roosevelt. *Trailing the Giant Panda.* New York, 1929; 278 pp.

Scott, Erastus H. *Travel Letters from the Orient.* [Chicago, 1922]; 84 pp.

Speakman, Harold. *Beyond Shanghai.* New York, 1922; 198 pp.

Sprague, Roger. *From Western China to the Golden Gate; The Experiences of an American University Graduate in the Orient.* Berkeley, 1911; 128 pp.

Steele, James King. *Wandering Feet along Well-known Highways and Unfrequented Byways of China and Japan: A Collection of Travel Sketches.* San Francisco, 1923; 301 pp.

Tinling, Christine I. *Bits of China; Travel-sketches in the Orient.* New York, 1925; 222 pp.

Tracy, Jane Allyn. *See China with Me.* Boston, 1930; 216 pp.

2.2   MERCHANTS AND ENTREPRENEURS
BIOGRAPHICAL COLLECTIONS

Barrett, Walter [Joseph A. Scoville]. *The Old Merchants of New York City.* New York, 1863–1870; 5 vols.

Hunt, Freeman, ed. *Lives of American Merchants.* New York, 1858; 2 vols.

State Street Trust Company. *Other Merchants and Sea Captains of Old Boston* . . . Boston, 1919; 70 pp.

State Street Trust Company. *Some Merchants and Sea Captains of Old Boston* . . . Boston, 1918; 53 pp.

1784–1900

[Appleton, William] Robbins, Chandler. "Memoir of Hon. William Appleton," Massachusetts Historical Society, *Proceedings,* 6:430–465 (1862–1863).

[Astor, John Jacob] Porter, Kenneth Wiggins. *John Jacob Astor, Business Man.* Cambridge, Mass., 1931; 2 vols.

Bickmore, Albert S. *Sketch of a Journey from Canton to Hankow Through China.* New Haven, [1868]; 19 pp.

[Cabot, George] Lodge, Henry Cabot. *Life and Letters of George Cabot.* Boston, 1877; 615 pp.

[Cabot family] Briggs, Lloyd Vernon. *History and Genealogy of the Cabot Family, 1475–1927.* Boston, 1927; 2 vols.

[Codman, John] "Captain Codman on Yankee Traders and Elephants," *American Neptune,* 2:271–277 (1942).

[Cushing, John Perkins] Larson, Henrietta M. "A China Trader Turns Investor — A Biographical Chapter in

American Business History," *Harvard Business Review*, 12:345–358 (1933–1934).

[Delano family] Delano, Daniel W., Jr. *Franklin Roosevelt and the Delano Influence*. Pittsburgh, 1946; 368 pp.

[Dorr, Sullivan] Corning, Howard. "Sullivan Dorr, An Early China Merchant: Extracts from a Notebook Kept by Him in Canton, 1801," Essex Institute, *Historical Collections*, 78:158–175 (1942).

[Dorr, Sullivan] Corning, Howard. "Sullivan Dorr, China Trader," *Rhode Island History*, 3:75–90 (1944).

[Dutilh family] Rau, Louise. "Dutilh Papers," Business Historical Society, *Bulletin*, 13:73–74 (1939).

[Forbes, John Murray] *Some Random Recollections of an Octogenarian*. Boston, 1898; 11 pp.

[Forbes, John Murray] Hughes, Sarah Forbes, ed. *Letters and Recollections of John Murray Forbes*. Boston, 1899; 2 vols.

[Forbes, John Murray] Hughes, Sarah Forbes, ed. *Letters (Supplementary) of John Murray Forbes*. Boston, 1905; 3 vols.

[Forbes, John Murray] Hughes, Sarah Forbes, ed. *Reminiscences of John Murray Forbes*. Boston, 1902; 3 vols.

[Forbes, John Murray] Pearson, Henry Greenleaf. *An American Railroad Builder, John Murray Forbes*. Boston, 1911; 196 pp.

Forbes, Robert B. "Personal Memoranda," Massachusetts Historical Society, *Proceedings*, 7:410–417 (1863–1864).

Forbes, Robert B. *Personal Reminiscences*. Boston, 1876; 382 pp.

[Forbes, Robert Bennet] Connolly, James B. *Canton Captain*. Garden City, N.Y., 1942; 342 pp.

[Gray, William] Gray, Edward. *William Gray, A Salem Merchant, A Biographical Sketch.* Boston, 1914; 124 pp.

Grew, Henry Sturgis. *Letters from China and Manila Written by Henry Sturgis Grew to His Parents, 1855 to 1862.* [Paris], 1927; 137 pp.

[Heard, Augustine] Corning, Howard. "Augustine Heard and the China Trade in the 1830's," Essex Institute, *Historical Collections,* 80:270–282 (1944).

[Heard, Augustine] Waters, Thomas Franklin. *Augustine Heard and His Friends.* [Salem, Mass.], 1916; 108 pp.

[Heard, John, III] Bishop, Elsie Hight. "The Business Man as a Business Historian," Business Historical Society, *Bulletin,* 12:17–24 (1938).

[Hill, Samuel] Snyder, James W., Jr., ed. "Voyage of the *Ophelia* from Boston to Canton: Excerpts from the Journal of Captain Samuel Hill," *New England Quarterly,* 10:355–380 (1937).

[Hill, Samuel] Snyder, James W., Jr., ed. "Voyage of the Ship 'Packet' to South America and China, 1817. (From the Journal of Captain Samuel Hill, Written at Sea)," *Americana,* 33:310–325 (1939).

Hunter, William C. *Bits of Old China.* London, 1885; 280 pp.

[Hunter, William C.] *The "Fan Kwae" at Canton before Treaty Days, 1825–1844.* London, 1882; 157 pp.

Ireland, John B. *Wall-street to Cashmere: A Journal of Five Years in Asia, Africa, and Europe . . .* New York, 1859; 531 pp.

[Jenckes, Edwin T.] Tanner, Earl C. "The Early Career of Edwin T. Jenckes, A Florida Pioneer of the 1830's," Florida Historical *Quarterly,* 30:261–275 (1951–1952).

[Kinsman, Abbot] "Excerpts from the Diary and the Letters of Abbot Kinsman from San Francisco, the Pacific,

Hong Kong and the Philippines," Essex Institute, *Historical Collections*, 89:72–93, 141–162 (1953).

[Kinsman, Nathaniel] Munroe, Mary Kinsman. "Nathaniel Kinsman, Merchant of Salem, in the China Trade, From the Kinsman Family Manuscripts," Essex Institute, *Historical Collections*, 85:9–40, 101–142 (1949).

[Kinsman, Rebecca Chase] "Journal of Rebecca Chase Kinsman Kept on her Voyage to China in 1843," Essex Institute, *Historical Collections*, 90:289–308, 389–409 (1954).

[Kinsman, Rebecca Chase] "Life in Macao in the 1840's; Letters of Rebecca Chase Kinsman to her Family in Salem," Essex Institute, *Historical Collections*, 86:15–40, 106–142, 257–284, 311–330 (1950); 87:114–149, 269–305, 388–409 (1951); 88:18–99 (1952).

[Low, Abiel Abbot] *Tribute of the Chamber of Commerce of the State of New York to the Memory of Abiel Abbot Low, President, 1863–1867*. New York, 1893; 29 pp.

[Low, William Henry] Phillips, James Duncan, ed. "The Canton Letters, 1839–1841, of William Henry Low," Essex Institute, *Historical Collections*, 84:197–228, 304–330 (1948).

[Low family] Augur, Helen. *Tall Ships to Cathay*. Garden City, N.Y., 1951; 255 pp.

[Low family] Loines, Elma, ed. *The China Trade Postbag of the Seth Low Family of Salem and New York, 1829–1873*. Manchester, Me., 1953; 324 pp.

[Low family] Loines, Elma, ed. "More Canton Letters of Abiel Abbot Low, William Henry Low, and Edward Allen Low (1837–1844)," Essex Institute, *Historical Collections*, 85:215–244 (1949).

Morris, Grace Parker. "Some Letters from 1792–1800 on the China Trade," *Oregon Historical Quarterly*, 42:48–87 (1941).

[Morris, Robert] Oberholtzer, Ellis Paxon. *Robert Morris, Patriot and Financier.* New York, 1903; 372 pp.

Nichols, George. *George Nichols, Salem Shipmaster and Merchant. An Autobiography,* ed. Martha Nichols. Salem, Mass., [1914]; 89 pp.

Nye, Gideon, Jr. *The Morning of My Life in China. Comprising an Outline of the History of Foreign Intercourse from . . . 1833 to . . . 1839.* Canton, 1873; 73 pp.

[Orne, William] Phillips, James Duncan. "William Orne, A Distinguished but Forgotten Merchant," Massachusetts Historical Society, *Proceedings,* 67:168–177 (1941–1944).

Parsons, William Barclay. *An American Engineer in China.* New York, 1900; 321 pp.

[Perkins, James] Perkins, Charles C. "Memoir of James Perkins," Massachusetts Historical Society, *Proceedings,* 1:353–368 (1791–1835).

[Perkins, Thomas Handasyd] Cary, Thomas G. *Memoir of Thomas Handasyd Perkins; Containing Extracts from His Diaries and Letters.* Boston, 1856; 304 pp.

[Perkins, Thomas Handasyd] Cary, Thomas G. "Thomas Handasyd Perkins," *New England Historical and Genealogical Register,* 10:201–211 (1856).

[Perkins, Thomas Handasyd] Hewes, Edwin B. "Thomas Handasyd Perkins, Supercargo of the *Astrea* of Salem," Essex Institute, *Historical Collections,* 71:203–215 (1935).

[Prescott, James S.] Stackpole, Edouard A. *Captain Prescott and the Opium Smugglers.* Mystic, Conn., 1954; 78 pp.

[Roundy, Henry] Lovett, Robert W. "American Merchant, Roundy," Essex Institute, *Historical Collections,* 97:61–78 (1961).

[Russell, George Robert] Lyman, Theodore. "Memoir of George Robert Russell, LL.D.," Massachusetts Historical Society, *Proceedings,* 18:280–281 (1880–1881).

Shaw, Samuel. *The Journals of Major Samuel Shaw, the First American Consul at Canton. With a Life of the Author by Josiah Quincy.* Boston, 1847; 360 pp.

Silsbee, Nathaniel. "Biographical Notes: Nathaniel Silsbee," Essex Institute, *Historical Collections,* 35:1–79 (1899).

[Snow, Samuel] Carosso, Vincent P., ed. "The Samuel Snow-Sullivan Dorr Correspondence," *Rhode Island History,* 15:65–88 (1956).

[Sturgis, Josiah] *A Brief Sketch of the Character and Services of Capt. Josiah Sturgis of the United States Revenue Service.* Boston, 1844; 34 pp.

[Sturgis, Russell] Sturgis, Julian. *From Books and Papers of Russell Sturgis.* Oxford, [1893?]; 272 pp.

[Sturgis, William] Larson, Henrietta M. "William Sturgis, Merchant and Investor," Business Historical Society, *Bulletin,* 9:76–77 (1935).

[Sturgis, William] Loring, Charles G. "Memoir of the Hon. William Sturgis," Massachusetts Historical Society, *Proceedings,* 7:420–473 (1863–1864).

[Swift, John White] "[Letter] John White Swift, Purser of the 'Empress of China,' the first vessel to sail from the United States to Canton, to his father, John Swift, of Philadelphia," *Pennsylvania Magazine of History and Biography,* 9:485 (1885–1886).

Tarrant, William. *Ningpo to Shanghai in 1857 via the Borders of Anwhui Province, Hoo-chow-foo and the Grand Canal.* Canton, 1862; 112 pp.

[Thompson, Alpheus Basil] Brown, Donald Mackenzie, ed. *China Trade Days in California; Selected Letters from the Thompson Papers, 1832–1863*. Berkeley, 1947; 94 pp.

Tiffany, Osmond, Jr. *The Canton Chinese; Or, The American's Sojourn in the Celestial Empire*. Boston, 1849; 271 pp.

[Tilden, Bryant Parrot] Jenkins, Lawrence Waters, ed. "An Old Mandarin Home," Essex Institute, *Historical Collections*, 71:103–119 (1935).

Train, George Francis. *An American Merchant in Europe, Asia, and Australia: A Series of Letters from Java, Singapore, China* . . . New York, 1857; 512 pp.

[Vanderford, Captain Benjamin] Dodge, Ernest S. "Captain Benjamin Vanderford of Salem," Essex Institute, *Historical Collections*, 79:315–329 (1943).

[Ward, Thomas W.] " 'Remarks on the Canton Trade and the Manner of Transacting Business.' From a Manuscript of 1809 in the Peabody Museum of Salem," Essex Institute, *Historical Collections*, 73:303–310 (1937).

Wetmore, William Shepard. *Recollections of Life in the Far East*. Shanghai, 1894; 60 pp.

Wilson, James Harrison. *China: Travels and Investigations in the "Middle Kingdom"* . . . New York, 1887; 376 pp.

1901–1949

Crow, Carl. *Four Hundred Million Customers, the Experiences . . . of an American in China* . . . New York, 1937; 316 pp.

[Davison, Henry Pomeroy] Lamont, Thomas W. *Henry P. Davison, The Record of a Useful Life*. New York, 1933; 373 pp.

[Dollar, Robert] *Private Diary of Robert Dollar on His Recent Visit to China* [San Francisco, 1912]; 210 pp.

[Harriman, Edward Henry] Kennan, George. *E. H. Harriman, a Biography.* Boston, 1922; 2 vols.

Hoover, Herbert. *Memoirs.* New York, 1951–1952; 3 vols.

Hutchison, James Lafayette. *China Hand.* Boston, 1936; 418 pp.

Lamont, Thomas William. *Across World Frontiers.* New York, 1951; 278 pp.

[Schiff, Jacob Henry] Adler, Cyrus. *Jacob H. Schiff; His Life and Letters.* Garden City, N.Y., 1928; 2 vols.

[Straight, Willard Dickerman] Croly, Herbert. *Willard Straight.* New York, 1924; 569 pp.

Thomas, James A. *A Pioneer Tobacco Merchant in the Orient.* Durham, N.C., 1928; 339 pp.

2.3 MISSIONARIES
PROTESTANT MISSIONARIES
Biographical collections: general

Beach, Harlan P. *Princely Men in the Heavenly Kingdom.* Boston, 1903; 224 pp.

Dean, William. *China Mission; Embracing a History of the Various Missions of All Denominations among the Chinese, with Biographical Sketches of Deceased Missionaries.* New York, 1859; 396 pp.

Forsyth, Robert Coventry, comp. and ed. *The China Martyrs of 1900; A Complete Roll of the Christian Heroes Martyred in China in 1900, with Narratives of Survivors.* New York, [1904]; 516 pp.

Gracey, Annie [Ryder]. *Eminent Missionary Women.* New York, 1898; 215 pp.

Ketler, Isaac C. *The Tragedy of Paotingfu: An Authentic*

Story of the Lives, Services and Sacrifices of the Presbyterian, Congregational and China Inland Missionaries Who Suffered Martyrdom at Paotingfu, China, June 30 and July 1, 1900. New York, 1902; 408 pp.

Lambert, John C. *Missionary Heroes in Asia; True Stories of the Intrepid Bravery and Stirring Adventures of Missionaries with Uncivilized Men, Wild Beasts and the Forces of Nature.* Philadelphia, 1908; 157 pp.

Mathews, Basil J., and Arthur E. Southon. *Torchbearers in China.* New York, 1924; 186 pp.

Memorials of Protestant Missionaries to the Chinese; Giving a List of Their Publications, and Obituary Notices of the Deceased. Shanghai, 1867; 331 pp.

Montgomery, Helen Barrett. *Western Women in Eastern Lands; an Outline Study of Fifty Years of Women's Work in Foreign Missions.* New York, 1911; 286 pp.

Mueller, John Theodore. *Great Missionaries to China.* Grand Rapids, 1947; 135 pp.

Mueller, John Theodore. *Great Missionaries to the Orient.* Grand Rapids, 1948; 133 pp.

Pierson, Hamilton Wilcox, ed. *American Missionary Memorial, Including Biographical and Historical Sketches.* New York, 1853; 504 pp.

Sallee, Annie [Jenkins]. *Torchbearers in Honan.* Nashville, 1948; 192 pp.

Speer, Robert E. *Servants of the King.* New York, 1909; 216 pp.

Trumbull, Henry Clay. *Old Time Student Volunteers; My Memories of Missionaries.* New York, 1902; 281 pp.

Wiley, Isaac William, ed. *The Mission Cemetery and the Fallen Missionaries of Fuh Chau China.* New York, [1858]; 374 pp.

Biographical collections: denominational

[China Inland Mission] Broomhall, Marshall, ed. *Martyred Missionaries of the China Inland Mission; With a Record of the Perils & Sufferings of Some Who Escaped.* New York, 1901; 329 pp.

[China Inland Mission] Broomhall, Marshall. *Pioneer Work in Hunan by Adam Dorward and Other Missionaries of the China Inland Mission.* Philadelphia, 1906; 113 pp.

[Church of the Nazarene] Hinshaw, Amy N. *Messengers of the Cross in China.* Kansas City, Mo., [1931?]; 118 pp.

[(Congregational) American Board of Commissioners for Foreign Missions] Blodget, Henry, and C. C. Baldwin. *Sketches of the Missions of the American Board in China.* Boston, 1896; 57 pp.

[Disciples of Christ] *They Went to China: Biographies of Missionaries of the Disciples of Christ.* [Indianapolis, 1948]; 95 pp.

[Lutheran] *Our Second Decade in China, 1915–1925; Sketches and Reminiscences by Missionaries of the Augustana Synod Mission in the Province of Honan.* n.p., [1925?]; 224 pp.

[Reformed Church in the United States] Good, James Isaac. *Famous Missionaries of the Reformed Church.* Philadelphia, 1903; 410 pp.

1830–1900

Abeel, David. *Journal of a Residence in China and the Neighboring Countries from 1829 to 1833.* New York, 1834; 398 pp.

[Abeel, David] Williamson, G. R. *Memoir of the Rev.*

David Abeel, D.D., Late Missionary to China. New York, 1848; 315 pp.

[Aitchison, William] Bush, Charles P. *Five Years in China; or, The Factory Boy Made a Missionary.* Philadelphia, [1865]; 284 pp.

[Aldersey, Mary Ann] Gracey, Annie [Ryder]. *Eminent Missionary Women.* New York, 1898; 215 pp.

Allen, Young J. *The Diary of a Voyage to China, 1859–1860,* ed. Arva Colbert Floyd. Atlanta, 1943; 39 pp.

[Allen, Young J.] Candler, Warren A. *Young J. Allen, "The Man Who Seeded China."* Nashville, 1931; 245 pp.

[Allen, Young J.] Loehr, George R. "Young J. Allen and Mandarins," *Emory University Quarterly,* 4:102–109 (1948).

[Ament, William Scott] Porter, Henry D. *William Scott Ament, Missionary of the American Board to China.* New York, 1911; 377 pp.

[Bonafield, Julia] Cowen, Mrs. B. R. *History of the Cincinnati Branch, Women's Foreign Missionary Society, 1869–1894.* Cincinnati, 1895; 160 pp.

Bridgman, Elijah Coleman. *Letters to Children from China.* Boston, 1834; 130 pp.

[Bridgman, Elijah Coleman] Bridgman, Eliza Jane [Gillett]. *Pioneer of American Missions in China; The Life and Labours of Elijah Coleman Bridgman.* New York, 1864; 296 pp.

[Bridgman, Elijah Coleman] Stifler, Susan R. "Elijah Coleman Bridgman; The First American Sinologist," *Notes on Far Eastern Studies in America* . . . 10:1–11 (1942).

[Brown, Samuel Robbins] Griffis, William Elliot. *A Maker of the New Orient, Samuel Robbins Brown,*

Pioneer Educator in China, America, and Japan. New York, 1902; 332 pp.

[Dean, Theodosia Ann Barker] Church, Pharcellus. *Notices of the Life of Theodosia Ann Barker Dean, Wife of Rev. William Dean, Missionary to China.* Boston, 1851; 288 pp.

[Doolittle, Justus] Blatt, Marilyn. "Problems of a China Missionary — Justus Doolittle," *Papers on China,* 12:28–50 (1958).

[Doolittle, Justus] Trumbull, Henry Clay. *Old Time Student Volunteers: My Memories of Missionaries.* New York, 1902; 281 pp.

[Fay, Lydia Mary] Gracey, Annie [Ryder]. *Eminent Missionary Women.* New York, 1898; 215 pp.

Gould, Annie Allender. *See* Mary S. Morrill.

Graves, Roswell H. *Forty Years in China; Or, China in Transition.* Baltimore, 1895; 316 pp.

[Green, Samuel Fisk] Cutler, Ebenezer, comp. *Life and Letters of Samuel Fisk Green . . . of Green Hill,* n.p., 1891; 456 pp.

[Happer, Andrew P.] Trumbull, Henry Clay. *Old Time Student Volunteers: My Memories of Missionaries.* New York, 1902; 281 pp.

[Haygood, Laura Askew] Brown, Oswald Eugene, and Anna Muse. *Life and Letters of Laura Askew Haygood.* Nashville, 1904; 522 pp.

[Hodge, C. Van R.] Speer, Robert E. *Young Men Who Overcame.* New York, 1905; 229 pp.

[Hoy, William Edwin] Good, James Isaac. *Famous Missionaries of the Reformed Church.* Philadelphia, 1903; 410 pp.

[Ingle, James Addison] Jefferys, William Hamilton. *James Addison Ingle (Yin Teh-sen) First Bishop of the Mis-*

sionary District of Hankow, China. New York, 1913; 286 pp.

[Keith, Caroline Phebe (Tenney)] Tenney, William C., ed. *Memoir of Mrs. Caroline P. Keith, Missionary of the Protestant Episcopal Church to China.* New York, 1864; 392 pp.

[Lambuth, James William] *In Memoriam: James William Lambuth . . . Veteran Missionary of China, Founder of the Southern Methodist Mission of Japan.* [Kobe, Japan, 1892]; 77 pp.

[Leffingwell, Clara] Sellew, Walter A. *Clara Leffingwell, A Missionary.* Chicago, 1907; 320 pp.

[Lord, Lucy T. (Lyon)] *Memoir of Mrs. Lucy T. Lord, of the Chinese Baptist Mission.* Philadelphia, 1854; 288 pp.

[Lowrie, Walter Macon] Lowrie, Walter, ed. *Memoirs of the Rev. Walter M. Lowrie, Missionary to China.* New York, 1850; 504 pp.

[Marshall, Elsie] *"For His Sake." A Record of a Life Consecrated to God and Devoted to China. Extracts from the Letters of Elsie Marshall, Martyred at Hwa-sang, August 1, 1895.* New York, 1896; 223 pp.

Martin, William Alexander Parsons. *A Cycle of Cathay: Or, China, South and North, With Personal Reminiscences.* New York, 1896; 464 pp.

[Martin, William Alexander Parsons] Duus, Peter. "Science and Salvation in China: The Life and Work of W. A. P. Martin," *Papers on China,* 10:97–127 (1956).

[Martin, William Alexander Parsons] Farquhar, Norma. "A Bibliography of the Writings of W. A. P. Martin," *Papers on China,* 10:128–141 (1956).

[Mateer, Calvin Wilson] Fisher, Daniel Webster. *Calvin Wilson Mateer, Forty-five Years a Missionary in Shan-*

tung, China; A Biography. Philadelphia, 1911; 342 pp.

[Mateer, Julia (Brown)] Mateer, Robert McCheyne. *Character-building in China; The Life-story of Julia Brown Mateer*. New York, 1912; 184 pp.

[Morrill, Mary S.] Kyle, Alice M., ed. *In Memory of Miss Mary S. Morrill and Miss Annie Allender Gould, Martyrs of Paoting-fu, North China, July 1, 1900*. Boston, n.d.; 116 pp.

Nevius, Helen Sanford [Coan]. *Our Life in China*. New York, 1869; 504 pp.

[Nevius, John Livingston] Nevius, Helen Sanford [Coan]. *The Life of John Livingston Nevius, for Forty Years a Missionary in China*. New York, 1895; 476 pp.

[Nicholson, Jennie Hughes] White, Mary Culler. *Days of June; the Life Story of June Nicholson*. New York, 1909; 128 pp.

[Pilcher, Leander William] Pilcher, Lewis S. *A Memorial of Leander William Pilcher, President of Peking University, and Missionary of the Methodist Episcopal Church to China*. n.p., 1895; 40 pp.

[Pitkin, Horace Tracy] Speer, Robert E. *A Memorial of Horace Tracy Pitkin*. New York, 1903; 310 pp.

[Pitkin, Horace Tracy] Speer, Robert E. *Young Men Who Overcame*. New York, 1905; 229 pp.

[Rankin, Dora] Fielder, Elizabeth Davis, comp. *Dora Rankin, In Memoriam*. Nashville, 1899; 93 pp.

[Schereschewsky, Samuel Isaac Joseph] Muller, James Arthur. *Apostle of China; Samuel Isaac Joseph Schereschewsky, 1831–1906*. Milwaukee, 1937; 279 pp.

[Sheffield, Devello Z.] Paterno, Roberto. "Devello Z. Sheffield, and the Founding of the North China College," *Papers on China*, 14:110–160 (1960).

[Shuck, Henrietta (Hall)] Dunaway, Thomas S. *Pioneer-*

ing for Jesus, the Story of Henrietta Hall Shuck. Nashville, [1930]; 160 pp.

[Shuck, Henrietta (Hall)] Jeter, Jeremiah Bell. *A Memoir of Mrs. Henrietta Shuck, the First American Female Missionary to China.* Boston, 1849; 251 pp.

[Speer, William] Trumbull, Henry Clay. *Old Time Student Volunteers: My Memories of Missionaries.* New York, 1902; 281 pp.

Stott, Grace [Ciggie]. *Twenty-six Years of Missionary Work in China,* 2d ed. New York, 1897; 366 pp.

[Talmage, John Van Nest] Fagg, John Gerardus. *Forty Years in South China; The Life of Rev. John Van Nest Talmage.* New York, 1894; 301 pp.

[White, Jane Isabel (Atwater)] Pierson, Hamilton Wilcox, ed. *American Missionary Memorial, Including Biographical and Historical Sketches,* New York, 1853; 504 pp.

Wiley, Isaac William. *China and Japan; A Record of Observations Made During a Residence of Several Years in China, and a Tour of Official Visitation to the Missions of Both Countries in 1877–78.* Cincinnati, 1879; 548 pp.

Williams, Isabella Riggs. *By the Great Wall; Letters from China; The Selected Correspondence of Isabella Riggs Williams, Missionary of the American Board to China, 1866–1879.* New York, 1909; 400 pp.

[Williams, Samuel Wells] Williams, Frederick Wells. *The Life and Letters of Samuel Wells Williams, LL.D., Missionary, Diplomatist, Sinologue.* New York, 1889; 490 pp.

[Williams, Samuel Wells] Latourette, Kenneth S. "Samuel Wells Williams (1812–84)," *Notes on Far Eastern Studies in America,* No. 12:4–8 (1943).

Williamson, Isabelle. *Old Highways in China*. New York, n.d.; 293 pp.

Wilson, Mrs. Alpheus Waters. *Letters from the Orient to her Daughters at Home*. Nashville, 1890; 253 pp.

[Woolston, Beulah] Gracey, Annie [Ryder]. *Eminent Missionary Women*. New York, 1898; 215 pp.

[Yates, Matthew Tyson] Speer, Robert E. *Servants of the King*. New York, 1909; 216 pp.

[Yates, Matthew Tyson] Taylor, Charles E. *The Story of Yates the Missionary, as Told in his Letters and Reminiscences*. Nashville, 1898; 304 pp.

[Yates, Matthew Tyson and Eliza Morning] *At the Gates; Life Story of Matthew Tyson and Eliza Morning Yates of China*. Nashville, [1914]; 374 pp.

1901–1949

[Adams, Joseph Samuel] Adams, Archibald Guinness. "Joseph Samuel Adams of China, an Original Contribution to the History of Protestant World Missions in the Form of a Biographical Record of the Missionary Career of his Father." Th.D. thesis, Union Theological Seminary, 1939; 2 vols.

[Anglin, Leslie M.] Albus, Harry James. *Twentieth-Century Onesiphorus; The Story of Leslie M. Anglin and the Home of Onesiphorus*. Grand Rapids, 1951; 160 pp.

[Atkinson, Virginia M.] White, Mary Culler, *Just Jennie; The Life Story of Virginia M. Atkinson*. Atlanta, 1955; 103 pp.

Bacon, Bessie [Blanchard]. *"With Heaps o' Love"; The Story of Four Years in China, Told in Letters*, ed. Charles Blanchard. Des Moines, 1925; 288 pp.

[Bashford, James Whitford] Grose, George Richmond.

James W. Bashford, Pastor, Educator, Bishop. New York, 1922; 252 pp.

Beckman, Erik Richard. *The Massacre at Sianfu and Other Experiences in Connection with the Scandinavian Alliance Mission of North America.* Chicago, 1913; 138 pp.

[Borden, William Whiting] Taylor, Mary Geraldine [Guinness]. *Borden of Yale '09; "The Life that Counts."* London, 1926; 287 pp.

Brockman, Fletcher Sims. *I Discover the Orient.* New York, 1935; 211 pp.

Brockway, Alice [Pickford]. *Letters from the Far East.* Philadelphia, 1919; 75 pp.

Brodbeck, Emma. *Chicago Missionary on the Burma Road; Letters of Emma Brodbeck, Ipin, Szechwan, West China.* [Chicago], 1941; 35 pp.

[Brown, Charlotte (Thompson)] Brown, Frank A. *Charlotte Brown, A Mother in China; The Story of the Work of Charlotte Thompson Brown in China from 1904–1949.* n.p., 1953; 100 pp.

[Bryan, Robert Thomas] Bryan, F. Catharine. *His Golden Cycle; The Life Story of Robert Thomas Bryan.* Richmond, Va., 1938; 297 pp.

Bryson, Arnold G. "Then and Now: Twenty Years in an Up-country Mission Station," *Chinese Recorder,* 54:257–261 (1923).

Bugge, Sten. "Selections from the Diary of a Travelling Evangelist," *Chinese Recorder,* 53:586–592 (1922).

[Burke, William B.] Burke, James C. *My Father in China.* New York, 1942; 431 pp.

Caldwell, Harry R. *Blue Tiger.* New York, 1924; 261 pp.

Caldwell, John Cope. *China Coast Family.* Chicago, 1953; 228 pp.

[Chambers, Robert Edward] Gardner, Ruth [Carver], and

Christine [Coffee] Chambers. *Builder of Dreams; The Life of Robert Edward Chambers.* Nashville, [1939]; 200 pp.

Chaplin, Maxwell. *The Letters of Maxwell Chaplin,* ed. George Stewart. New York, 1928; 239 pp.

Clayton, Edward Hyers. *Heaven Below.* New York, 1944; 282 pp.

[Corbett, Hunter] Craighead, James R. E. *Hunter Corbett: Fifty-six Years a Missionary in China.* New York, [1921]; 224 pp.

Corey, Stephen J. *Among Asia's Needy Millions . . . Journal of a Visit to the Far East.* Cincinnati, 1915; 255 pp.

[Crawford, Tarleton Perry] Foster, Lovelace Savidge. *Fifty Years in China; An Eventful Memoir of Tarleton Perry Crawford.* Nashville, 1909; 361 pp.

Cressy, Earl Herbert. *Yellow Rivers; Adventures in a Chinese Parish.* New York, 1932; 153 pp.

Cushman, Clara M. *Tientsin Scribbles.* Leominster, Mass., 1925; 221 pp.

Drach, George. *Seeing Things in the Far East. Incidents, Experiences and Observations of a Journey to India, China and Japan.* Baltimore, 1926; 166 pp.

Duncan, Marion Herbert. *The Mountain of Silver Snow.* Cincinnati, 1929; 240 pp.

Duncan, Marion Herbert. *The Yangtze and the Yak; Adventurous Trails In and Out of Tibet.* Alexandria, Va., 1952; 353 pp.

Eddy, George Sherwood. *Eighty Adventurous Years; An Autobiography.* New York, 1955; 255 pp.

Eddy, George Sherwood. *I Have Seen God Work in China; Personal Impressions from Three Decades with the Chinese.* New York, 1944; 137 pp.

Ekvall, Robert B. *Gateway to Tibet; The Kansu-Tibetan Border.* Harrisburg, Pa., [1938]; 198 pp.

[Farmer, Ada (Beeson)] Farmer, Wilmoth Alexander. *Ada Beeson Farmer, A Missionary Heroine of Kuang Si, South China.* Atlanta, 1912; 325 pp.

Fox, John. *Around the World for the American Bible Society; Being Twelve Letters Descriptive of a Visit to the Society's Agencies in the Far East.* New York, 1908; 47 pp.

[Franson, Frederick] Princell, Josephine. *Frederick Franson, World Missionary.* Chicago, n.d.; 156 pp.

Fridell, Elmer A. *You Too May Go. Excerpts from the Letters of Dr. Elmer A. Fridell . . . Written during a Year's Visit to the Philippine Islands, China and Japan from September 1945 to September 1946,* ed. Jesse R. Wilson. New York, 1947; 79 pp.

[Frost, Henry Weston] Taylor, Frederick Howard and Mary Geraldine [Guinness]. *"By Faith . . .": Henry W. Frost and the China Inland Mission.* Philadelphia, 1938; 365 pp.

Fulton, Mary H. *"Inasmuch." Extracts from Letters, Journals, Papers, etc.* West Medford, Mass., n.d.; 125 pp.

Gamewell, Mary [Porter]. *Mary Porter Gamewell and her Story of the Siege in Peking,* ed. Alexander Harrison Tuttle. New York, 1907; 303 pp.

Goddard, Francis Wayland. *Called to Cathay.* New York, [1948]; 159 pp.

[Goforth, Jonathan] Goforth, Rosalind [Bellsmith]. *Goforth of China.* Grand Rapids, 1937; 364 pp.

Goforth, Rosalind [Bellsmith], and Jonathan Goforth. *Miracle Lives of China.* New York, 1931; 157 pp.

[Gulick, John Thomas] Gulick, Addison. *Evolutionist and*

Missionary, John Thomas Gulick, Portrayed through Documents and Discussions. Chicago, 1932; 556 pp.

Heebner, Flora K. *Our Mission Work in Taiku, Shansi, China, Before and After the "Occupation," Containing the Story of the Repatriation; The Journal of Flora K. Heebner.* Philadelphia, 1942; 15 pp.

Honsinger, Welthy. *Beyond the Moon Gate: Being a Diary of Ten Years in the Interior of the Middle Kingdom.* New York, 1924; 176 pp.

Huizenga, Lee S. *Pressing On; An Autobiographical Sketch.* Grand Rapids, 1946; 83 pp.

[Huizenga, Lee S.] Lamberts, Lambertus J. *The Life Story of Dr. Lee S. Huizenga; An Adventure in Faith.* Grand Rapids, 1950; 194 pp.

[Jackson, Alice] Speer, Robert E. *A Memorial of Alice Jackson.* New York, 1908; 128 pp.

[Jaffray, Robert A.] Tozer, Aiden Wilson. *Let My People Go! The Life of Robert A. Jaffray.* Harrisburg, Pa., 1947; 127 pp.

[Landahl, Carl William] Burgess, Andrew S. *Lan Ta-tê. Landahl of China.* Minneapolis, [1941]; 116 pp.

[Luce, Henry Winters] Garside, Bettis Alston. *One Increasing Purpose; The Life of Henry Winters Luce.* New York, 1948; 271 pp.

Lundeen, Anton. *In the Grip of Bandits and Yet in the Hands of God.* [Rock Island, Ill.], 1925; 143 pp.

Mateer, Mrs. Ada Haven. *Siege Days; Personal Experiences of American Women and Children During the Peking Siege.* New York, 1903; 411 pp.

Melrose, Paul C. *On Being a Missionary.* New York, 1957; 73 pp.

[Moon, Lottie] Lawrence, Una [Roberts]. *Lottie Moon.* Nashville, 1927; 317 pp.

[Mott, John Raleigh] Mathews, Basil. *John R. Mott, World Citizen.* New York, 1934; 469 pp.

[Nelson, Bert N.] Nelson, Daniel. *The Apostle to the Chinese Communists.* Minneapolis, 1935; 139 pp.

Nelson, Daniel. *Journey to Chungking.* Minneapolis, 1945; 154 pp.

Nichols, Buford, L. *It Happened in China; Random Glimpses of Life in China* . . . Nashville, 1948; 100 pp.

Noyes, Harriet Newell. *A Light in the Land of Sinim; Forty-five Years in the True Light Seminary, 1872–1917.* New York, 1919; 250 pp.

Patterson, L. D. *If Two Agree.* Nashville, 1921; 102 pp.

Poteat, Gordon. *Home Letters from China; The Story of How a Missionary Found and Began his Life Work in the Heart of China.* New York, 1924; 159 pp.

[Pye, Watts O.] Schrecker, John. "Watts O. Pye, Missionary to China, 1907–1926," *Papers on China,* 13:32–60 (1959).

[Reimert, William Anson] Bartholomew, Allen R. *The Martyr of Huping; The Life Story of William Anson Reimert* . . . Philadelphia, 1925; 157 pp.

[Rønning, Halvor Nilson] Rønning, Halvor Nilson and Nils Nilsen. *The Gospel at Work.* Minneapolis, 1943; 127 pp.

[Sallee, W. Eugene] Sallee, Annie [Jenkins]. *W. Eugene Sallee, Christ's Ambassador.* Nashville, 1933; 256 pp.

Scott, Charles Ernest. *China from Within; Impressions and Experiences.* New York, 1917; 327 pp.

[Seabury, Warren Bartlett] Seabury, John Bartlett. *The Vision of a Short Life; A Memorial of Warren Bartlett Seabury, One of the Founders of the Yale Mission College in China.* Cambridge, Mass., 1909; 192 pp.

[Sites, Nathan] Sites, S. Moore. *Nathan Sites, an Epic of the East.* New York, 1912; 256 pp.

[Stam, John Cornelius] English, Eugene Schuyler. *By Life and by Death: Excerpts and Lessons from the Diary of John C. Stam.* Grand Rapids, [1938]; 62 pp.

[Stam, John Cornelius and Elizabeth Alden (Scott)] Huizenga, Lee S. *John and Betty Stam, Martyrs . . . A Short Story of the Life and Death of Mr. and Mrs. John C. Stam.* Grand Rapids, 1935; 64 pp.

[Stam, John Cornelius and Elizabeth Alden (Scott)] Taylor, Mary Geraldine [Guinness]. *The Triumph of John and Betty Stam.* Philadelphia, 1935; 125 pp.

Stuart, John Leighton. *Fifty Years in China: The Memoirs of John Leighton Stuart, Missionary and Ambassador.* New York, 1954; 346 pp.

[Sydenstricker, Absalom] Buck, Pearl [Sydenstricker]. *Fighting Angel; Portrait of a Soul.* New York, 1936; 302 pp.

[Sydenstricker, Caroline (Stulting)] Buck, Pearl [Sydenstricker]. *The Exile.* New York, 1936; 315 pp.

[Thurston, John Lawrence] Wright, Henry D. *A Life with a Purpose; A Memorial of John Lawrence Thurston, First Missionary of the Yale Mission.* New York, 1908; 317 pp.

[Troxel, Cecil Warren] Troxel, Ellen [Armour], and Mrs. John J. Trachsel. *Cecil Troxel, the Man and the Work.* Chicago, 1948; 261 pp.

Turner, William H. *Pioneering in China.* Franklin Springs, Ga., 1928; 312 pp.

Vaughan, Louisa. *Answered or Unanswered.* Wichita, Kan., 1917; 128 pp.

Wampler, Ernest M. *China Suffers; or, My Six Years of Work during the Incident.* Elgin, Ill., 1945; 277 pp.

[Williams, John Elias]. Wheeler, William Reginald. *John E. Williams of Nanking.* New York, 1937; 222 pp.

White, Mary Culler. *I Was There . . . When It Happened in China.* New York, 1947; 123 pp.

CATHOLIC MISSIONARIES
Biographical collections

Keller, James G., and Meyer Berger. *Men of Maryknoll.* New York, 1943; 191 pp.

Maryknoll Mission Letters — China; Extracts from the Letters and Diaries of the Pioneer Missioners of the Catholic Foreign Mission Society of America. New York, 1923 and 1927; 2 vols.

Individual biographies

[Cairns, Robert John] Reid, Richard, and Edward J. Moffett. *Three Days to Eternity; Being the Story of Father Sandy Cairns, Maryknoll Missioner and Modern Apostle.* Westminster, Md., 1956; 179 pp.

[Conley, Lawrence Aiden] Cosgrove, Joseph G. *Accent on Laughter; A Life Sketch of Father Lawrence A. Conley, M.M., Maryknoll Missioner in South China.* New York, 1952; 102 pp.

Cuenot, Joseph. *Kwangsi, Land of the Black Banners.* St. Louis, 1942; 279 pp.

[Donovan, Gerard Aloysius] Considine, John Joseph. *When the Sorghum Was High; A Narrative Biography of Father Gerard A. Donovan . . . a Maryknoll Missioner Slain by Bandits in Manchukuo.* New York, 1941; 177 pp.

[Engbring, Francis Xavier] Habig, Marion A. *Pioneering in China: The Story of the Rev. Francis Xavier Engbring, O.F.M., First Native American Priest in China,*

1857–1895, with Sketches of His Missionary Comrades. Chicago, 1930; 155 pp.

Ford, Francis Xavier. *Stone in the King's Highway; Selections from the Writings of Bishop Francis Xavier Ford (1892–1952).* New York, 1953; 297 pp.

Krock, George L. *Stop Killing Dragons; Letters to a Roman Knight from a Maryknoll Missioner.* [New York], 1947; 137 pp.

[McGlinchey, Henry P.] Boyton, Neil. *A Yankee Xavier: Henry P. McGlinchey, S.J.* New York, 1937; 137 pp.

[McShane, Daniel Leo] McShane, John Francis. *My Brother, the Maryknoll Missionary; A Life of the Rev. Daniel Leo McShane, M.M.* St. Meinrad, Ind., 1932; 116 pp.

[McShane, Daniel Leo] Walsh, James Edward. *Father McShane of Maryknoll, Missioner in South China.* New York, 1932; 227 pp.

Maguire, Theophane. *Hunan Harvest.* Milwaukee, 1946; 191 pp.

Mary Rosalia, Sister. *One Inch of Splendor.* New York, 1941; 90 pp.

[Price, Thomas Frederick] *Father Price of Maryknoll; A Short Sketch of the Life of Reverend Thomas Frederick Price, Missioner in North Carolina, Co-founder of Maryknoll, Missioner in China, Compiled from the Letters of his Friends,* ed. Patrick James Byrne. Maryknoll, N.Y., [1923]; 91 pp.

[Price, Thomas Frederick] Murrett, John C. *Tar Heel Apostle, Thomas Frederick Price, Cofounder of Maryknoll.* New York, 1944; 260 pp.

Tennien, Mark A. *Chungking Listening Post.* New York, 1945; 201 pp.

Walsh, James Anthony. *Observations in the Orient; the Account of a Journey to Catholic Mission Fields in Japan, Korea, Manchuria, China, Indo-China, and the Philippines,* Ossining, N.Y., 1919; 323 pp.

[Walsh, James Anthony] Sargent, Daniel. *All the Day Long: James Anthony Walsh, Cofounder of Maryknoll.* New York, 1941; 259 pp.

2.4 DOCTORS
BIOGRAPHICAL COLLECTIONS

Wang Chi-min. *Lancet and Cross; Biographical Sketches of Fifty Pioneer Medical Missionaries in China.* [Shanghai], 1950; 160 pp.

INDIVIDUAL BIOGRAPHIES

Adolph, Paul E. *Surgery Speaks to China; The Experiences of a Medical Missionary to China in Peace and War. Philadelphia,* 1945; 195 pp.

[Anderson, John Todd] Poteat, Gordon. *A Greatheart of the South, John T. Anderson, Medical Missionary.* New York, 1921; 123 pp.

Basil, George C., and Elizabeth Foreman Lewis. *Test Tubes and Dragon Scales.* Philadelphia, 1940; 316 pp.

[Bethune, Norman] Allan, Ted, and Sydney Gordon. *The Scalpel, the Sword; the Story of Dr. Norman Bethune.* Boston, 1952; 336 pp.

Bettelheim, Bernard Jean. *Letter from B. J. Bettelheim, M.D., Missionary in Lewchew, Addressed to Rev. Peter Parker, M.D.* Canton, 1852; 42 pp..

[DuBose, Hampden Coit and Pauline (McAlpine)] Junkin, Nettie [DuBose], comp. *For the Glory of God.*

Memoirs of Dr. and Mrs. H. C. DuBose of Soochow, China. Lewisburg, W.Va., [1915?]; 76 pp.

Dunlap, Albert M. *Behind the Bamboo Curtain; the Experiences of an American Doctor in China.* Washington, 1956; 208 pp.

Fearn, Anne Walter. *My Days of Strength; An American Woman Doctor's Forty Years in China.* New York, 1939; 297 pp.

Hamilton, Guy Wheeler and Pauline Ernst Hamilton. *China Two Generations Ago; A Family Sketch of Guy and Pauline Ernst Hamilton, Presbyterian Medical Missionaries in the Interior of North China.* Denver, 1957; 102 pp.

Harper, Mary McKibbin. *The Doctor Takes a Holiday, An Autobiographical Fragment.* Cedar Rapids, Ia., 1941; 349 pp.

[Henderson, James] *Life of James Henderson, M.D. . . . Medical Missionary to China.* New York, 1873; 196 pp.

Holman, Nellie [Pederson]. *My Most Unforgettable Patients.* New York, 1953; 119 pp.

Howard, Harvey J. *Ten Weeks with Chinese Bandits.* New York, 1926; 272 pp.

Hume, Edward H. *Doctors Courageous.* New York, 1950; 297 pp.

Hume, Edward H. *Doctors East, Doctors West; An American Physician's Life in China.* New York, 1946; 278 pp.

[Hume, Edward H.] Hume, Lotta Carswell. *Drama at the Doctor's Gate; the Story of Doctor Edward Hume of Yale-in-China.* New Haven, 1961; 160 pp.

Kinnean, Ella J. A letter concerning the revolution in Foochow, 1912. [Foochow, 1912]. 1 sheet available at HU:HL

Leavell, George W. *Some Fruits of the Gospel; Experi-*

ences of a Medical Missionary. Nashville, 1928; 120 pp.

[Lewis, Charles] Speer, Robert E. *"Lu Taifu," Charles Lewis, M.D., A Pioneer Surgeon in China.* New York, [1934]; 216 pp.

Loftis, Zenas Sanford. *A Message from Batang; The Diary of Z. S. Loftis, M.D., Missionary to Tibetans.* New York, 1911; 160 pp.

[McCartee, Divie Bethune] Speer, Robert E. *A Missionary Pioneer in the Far East; A Memorial of Divie Bethune McCartee.* New York, 1922; 224 pp.

[Macklin, William Edward] Eberle, Edith. *Macklin of Nanking.* St. Louis, 1936; 173 pp.

[Macklin, William Edward] Garst, Laura DeLany. *In the Shadow of the Drum Tower.* Cincinnati, 1911; 136 pp.

[Miller, Harry Willis] Moore, Raymond S. *China Doctor; the Life Story of Harry Willis Miller.* New York, 1961; 215 pp.

Osgood, Elliott I. *Breaking Down Chinese Walls, From a Doctor's Viewpoint.* New York, 1908; 217 pp.

Palmborg, Ross W. *China Letters, Seventh Day Baptist Medical Missionary to China, 1894–1940.* Plainfield, N.J., 1942; 278 pp.

[Parker, Peter] Stevens, George B., and William Fisher Marwick. *The Life, Letters, and Journals of the Rev. and Hon. Peter Parker . . .* Boston, 1896; 362 pp.

[Parker, Peter] Trumbull, Henry Clay. *Old Time Student Volunteers; My Memories of Missionaries.* New York, 1902; 281 pp.

[Pettus, Winston] Hume, Edward H. *Dauntless Adventurer; the Story of Dr. Winston Pettus.* New Haven, 1952; 195 pp.

Powell, Charles A. *Bound Feet.* Boston, 1938; 339 pp.

Powell, Lyle Stephenson. *A Surgeon in Wartime China.* Lawrence, Kan., 1946; 233 pp.

Rijnhart, Susie Carson. *With the Tibetans in Tent and Temple: Narrative of Four Years' Residence on the Tibetan Border, and of a Journey into the Far Interior.* Chicago, 1901; 400 pp.

Scovel, Myra, and Nelle Keys Bell. *The Chinese Ginger Jars.* New York, 1962; 189 pp.

Sharpe, William. *Brain Surgeon; The Autobiography of William Sharpe.* New York, 1952; 271 pp.

[Sheldon, Martha] Baker, F. J. *Dr. Martha Sheldon and her Siege of Tibet.* Boston, [1905]; 8 pp.

Shelton, Albert L. *Pioneering in Tibet; A Personal Record of Life and Experience in Mission Fields.* New York, 1921; 214 pp.

[Shelton, Albert Leroy] Shelton, Flora Beal. *Shelton of Tibet.* New York, 1923; 319 pp.

Shelton, Flora Beal. *Sunshine and Shadow on the Tibetan Border.* Cincinnati, 1912; 141 pp.

Skinsnes, Casper C., *Scalpel and Cross in Honan.* Minneapolis, 1952; 254 pp.

Wheeler, William Reginald. *Flight to Cathay; an Aerial Journey to Yale-in-China.* New Haven, 1949; 81 pp.

2.5 JOURNALISTS

Abend, Hallett E. *My Life in China, 1926–1941.* New York, 1943; 396 pp.

Alcott, Carroll Duard. *My War with Japan.* New York, 1943; 368 pp.

Booker, Edna Lee. *News Is My Job; A Correspondent in War-torn China.* New York, 1940; 375 pp.

Booker, Edna Lee, and John S. Potter. *Flight from China.* New York, 1945; 236 pp.

Carr, Harry. *Riding the Tiger; An American Newspaper Man in the Orient.* Boston, 1934; 262 pp.

Chamberlin, Wilbur J. *Ordered to China; Letters of Wilbur J. Chamberlin Written from China . . . during the Boxer Uprising of 1900 and the International Complications which Followed.* New York, 1903; 340 pp.

Gould, Randall. *China in the Sun.* New York, 1946; 403 pp.

Homer, Joy. *Dawn Watch in China.* Boston, 1941; 340 pp.

Powell, John B. "Missourians in China," *Missouri Historical Review,* 15:611–616 (1920–1921).

Powell, John B. *My Twenty-five Years in China.* New York, 1945; 436 pp.

Sheean, Vincent. *Personal History.* Garden City, N.Y., 1935; 403 pp.

Smedley, Agnes. *China Fights Back, An American Woman with the Eighth Route Army.* New York, 1938; 282 pp.

Snow, Edgar. *Journey to the Beginning.* New York, 1958; 434 pp.

Vaughn, Miles W. *Covering the Far East.* New York, 1936; 408 pp.

2.6 SCHOLARS AND WRITERS
BIOGRAPHICAL COLLECTIONS

Hummel, Arthur W. "Some American Pioneers in Chinese Studies," *Notes on Far Eastern Studies in America,* no. 9:1–6 (1941).

INDIVIDUAL BIOGRAPHIES

Andrews, Roy Chapman, and Yvette Borup Andrews. *Camps and Trails in China; a Narrative of Explora-*

tion, Adventure, and Sport in Little-known China.
New York, 1918; 334 pp.

Ayscough, Florence [Wheelock]. *A Chinese Mirror; Being
Reflections of the Reality Behind Appearance.* Boston,
[1925]; 464 pp.

[Ayscough, Florence (Wheelock)] MacNair, Harley Farnsworth, ed. *Florence Ayscough & Amy Lowell; Correspondence of a Friendship.* Chicago, 1945; 288 pp.

[Ayscough, Florence (Wheelock)] MacNair, Harley Farns-
worth, ed. *The Incomparable Lady; Tributes and
Other Memorabilia Pertaining to Florence Wheelock
Ayscough MacNair.* Chicago, 1946; 149 pp.

Band, Claire and William. *Two Years with the Chinese
Communists.* New Haven, 1948; 347 pp.

[Bishop, Carl Whiting] Wilbur, C. Martin. "Carl Whiting
Bishop, 1881–1942." *Far Eastern Quarterly,* 2:204–207
(1943).

Buck, Pearl [Sydenstricker]. *My Several Worlds; A Personal Record.* New York, 1954; 407 pp.

Dewey, John, and Alice Chipman Dewey. *Letters from
China and Japan,* ed. Evelyn Dewey. New York, 1920;
311 pp.

[Elisséeff, Serge] Reischauer, Edwin O. "Serge Elisséeff,"
Harvard Journal of Asiatic Studies, 20:1–35 (1957).

[Gilman, F. P.] Meany, Edmond S. "A Pioneer Professor's
Grave in China," *Washington Historical Quarterly,*
22:210–212 (1931).

Hahn, Emily. *China to Me, A Partial Autobiography.*
Garden City, N.Y., 1944; 429 pp.

Hobart, Alice Tisdale [Nourse]. *By the City of the Long
Sand; A Tale of New China.* New York, 1926; 329 pp.

[Hodous, Lewis] Porter, Lucius Chapin. "Lewis Hodous,

December 11, 1872–August 9, 1949," *Far Eastern Quarterly*, 10:63–68 (1950–1951).

Kates, George Norbert. *The Years That Were Fat; Peking, 1933–1940*. New York, 1952; 268 pp.

[Laufer, Berthold] Latourette, Kenneth Scott. "Biographical Memoir of Berthold Laufer, 1874–1934," National Academy of Sciences, *Biographical Memoirs*, 18:43–68 (1938).

[MacNair, Harley Farnsworth] Price, Maurice T. "Harley Farnsworth MacNair (July 22, 1891–June 22, 1947)," *Far Eastern Quarterly*, 8:45–63 (1948–1949).

Peck, Graham. *Through China's Wall*. Boston, 1940; 371 pp.

Peck, Graham. *Two Kinds of Time*. Boston, 1950; 725 pp.

Seton, Grace [Gallatin]. *Chinese Lanterns*. New York, 1924; 373 pp.

Waln, Nora. *The House of Exile*. Boston, 1933; 337 pp.

Warner, Langdon. *The Long Old Road in China*. Garden City, N.Y., 1926; 168 pp.

[Williams, Edward Thomas] Gale, Esson M. "Edward Thomas Williams, 1854–1944," *Far Eastern Quarterly*, 3:381–383 (1943–1944).

Willis, Bailey. *Friendly China; Two Thousand Miles Afoot among the Chinese*. Stanford, 1949; 312 pp.

2.7 DIPLOMATS AND CONSULS

The following list is mainly concerned with American envoys to China and with consular officials. Published materials on presidents and cabinet officers can be easily found in standard reference works.

Allman, Norwood F. *Shanghai Lawyer*. New York, 1943; 283 pp.

[Angell, James Burrill] Gale, Esson M. "President James

Burrill Angell's Diary, as United States Treaty Commissioner and Minister to China, 1880–1881," *Michigan Alumnus, Quarterly Review,* 49:195–208 (1942–1943).

[Avery, Benjamin Parke] May, Ernest R. "Benjamin Parke Avery, Including a Review of the Office of State Printer, 1850–72," *California Historical Society Quarterly,* 30: 125–149 (1951).

[Burlingame, Anson] Koo, Telly Howard. "The Life of Anson Burlingame." Ph.D. thesis, Harvard University, 1922: 244 pp.

[Burlingame, Anson] Williams, Frederick Wells. *Anson Burlingame and the First Chinese Mission to Foreign Powers.* New York, 1912; 370 pp.

[Caldwell, John Cope] Gayn, Mark J., and John Caldwell. *American Agent.* New York, 1947; 229 pp.

Conger, Sarah Pike. *Letters from China, with Particular Reference to the Empress Dowager and the Women of China.* Chicago, 1909; 392 pp.

[Cushing, Caleb] Fuess, Claude Moore. "Caleb Cushing, a Memoir," Massachusetts Historical Society, *Proceedings,* 64:440–447 (1930–1932).

[Cushing, Caleb] Fuess, Claude Moore. *The Life of Caleb Cushing.* New York, 1923; 2 vols.

Denby, Charles. *China and Her People; Being the Observations, Reminiscences, and Conclusions of an American Diplomat.* Boston, 1906; 2 vols.

Dunham, Donald C. *Envoy Unextraordinary.* New York, 1944; 166 pp.

Huntington-Wilson, Francis Mairs. *Memoirs of an Ex-Diplomat.* Boston, 1945; 373 pp.

[Hurley, Patrick Jay] Lohbeck, Don. *Patrick J. Hurley.* Chicago, 1956; 513 pp.

[Marshall, George Catlett] Frye, William. *Marshall, Citizen Soldier.* Indianapolis, 1947; 397 pp.

[Marshall, George Catlett] Payne, Pierre Stephen Robert. *The Marshall Story; A Biography of General George C. Marshall.* New York, 1951; 344 pp.

Phillips, William. *Ventures in Diplomacy.* [North Beverly, Mass.?], 1952; 464 pp.

Reinsch, Paul S. *An American Diplomat in China.* Garden City, N.Y., 1922; 396 pp.

[Reinsch, Paul Samuel] Kent, Alan E. "Down from the Ivory Tower: Paul Samuel Reinsch, Minister to China," *Wisconsin Magazine of History,* 35:114–118 (1951).

Roberts, Edmund. *Embassy to the Eastern Courts of Cochin-China, Siam, and Muscat; in the U.S. Sloop-of-war Peacock . . . during the Years 1832–3–4.* New York, 1837; 432 pp.

[Rockhill, William Woodville] Varg, Paul A. *Open Door Diplomat; The Life of W. W. Rockhill.* Urbana, Ill., 1952; 141 pp.

Stanton, Edwin F. *Brief Authority; Excursions of a Common Man in an Uncommon World.* New York, 1956; 290 pp.

[Straight, Willard Dickerman] Croly, Herbert. *Willard Straight.* New York, 1924; 569 pp.

Townsend, Ralph. *Ways That Are Dark; The Truth about China.* New York, 1933; 336 pp.

Wallace, Henry A., and Andrew J. Steiger. *Soviet Asia Mission.* New York, 1946; 254 pp.

Williams, Samuel Wells. "Narrative of the American Embassy to Peking," *Journal of the North-China Branch of the Royal Asiatic Society,* 1:315–349 (1858–1859).

[Williams, Samuel Wells] Williams, Frederick Wells.

"The Journal of S. Wells Williams, LL.D.," *Journal of the North-China Branch of the Royal Asiatic Society,* 42:1–232 (1911).

[Williams, Samuel Wells] Williams, Frederick Wells. *The Life and Letters of Samuel Wells Williams, LL.D., Missionary, Diplomatist, Sinologue.* New York, 1889; 490 pp.

Young, John Russell. *Men and Memoirs; Personal Reminiscences,* ed. May D. Russell Young. New York, 1901; 2 vols.

2.8 MILITARY MEN

Carlson, Evans Fordyce. *Twin Stars of China, A Behind-the-Scenes Story of China's Valiant Struggle for Existence, by a U.S. Marine Who Lived & Moved with the People.* New York, 1940; 331 pp.

Dewey, George. *Autobiography of George Dewey, Admiral of the Navy* . . . New York, 1913; 337 pp.

[Dewey, George] Dewey, Adelbert M., *The Life and Letters of Admiral Dewey from Montpelier to Manila* . . . New York, 1899; 559 pp.

Finney, Charles G. *The Old China Hands.* New York, 1961; 258 pp.

Johnston, James D. *China and Japan: Being a Narrative of the Cruise of the U.S. Steam-Frigate Powhatan, in the Years 1857, '58, '59, and '60* . . . Philadelphia, 1860; 448 pp.

[Kearny, Lawrence] Alden, Carroll Storrs. *Lawrence Kearny, Sailor Diplomat.* Princeton, 1936; 231 pp.

[Kearny, Lawrence] McSweeney, Edward F. "Lawrence Kearny — 1789–1868," American Irish Historical Society, *Journal,* 22:108–122 (1923).

[McGriffin, Philo Norton] Forrest, Earle R. "Captain

Philo McGriffin at the Battle of the Yalu," *American Neptune*, 8:267–278 (1948).

[Powell, William Henry] Pratt, Julius W., ed. "Our First 'War' in China: The Diary of William Henry Powell, 1856," *American Historical Review*, 53:776–786 (1947–1948).

Reynolds, John N. *Voyage of the U.S. Frigate Potomac, under Command of John Downes, During the Circumnavigation of the Globe, 1831–34.* New York, 1835; 560 pp.

[Stilwell, Joseph Warren] *The Stilwell Papers,* ed. Theodore H. White. New York, 1948; 357 pp.

Taussig, J. K. "Experiences During the Boxer Rebellion," United States Naval Institute, *Proceedings,* 53:403–420 (1927).

[Trenchard, Stephen Decatur] Maclay, Edgar Stanton, ed. "New Light on the 'Blood is Thicker than Water' Episode (From the Private Papers of the Late Rear Admiral Stephen Decatur Trenchard, U.S. Navy)," United States Naval Institute, *Proceedings,* 40:1085–1103 (1914).

Wilson, James Harrison. *Under the Old Flag.* New York, 1912; 2 vols.

Wood, William Maxwell. *Fankwei, or the San Jacinto in the Seas of India, China, and Japan.* New York, 1859; 545 pp.

2.9 AMERICANS IN THE SERVICE OF THE CHINESE GOVERNMENT

Arlington, Lewis Charles. *Through the Dragon's Eyes; Fifty Years' Experience of a Foreigner in the Chinese Government Service.* London, 1931; 348 pp.

Chennault, Claire Lee. *Way of a Fighter; The Memoirs*

of Claire Lee Chennault, ed. Robert Hotz. New York, 1949; 375 pp.

[Chennault, Claire Lee] Ayling, Keith. *Old Leatherface of the Flying Tigers; The Story of General Chennault.* Indianapolis, 1945; 274 pp.

[Chennault, Claire Lee] Chennault, Anna. *A Thousand Springs: The Biography of a Marriage.* New York, 1962; 318 pp.

[Chennault, Claire Lee] Scott, Robert Lee. *Flying Tiger: Chennault of China.* Garden City, N.Y.; 285 pp.

Gale, Esson M. *Salt for the Dragon; A Personal History of China, 1908–1945.* [East Lansing, Mich.], 1953; 225 pp.

[Lea, Homer] Stimson, Marshall. "A Los Angeles Jeremiah; Homer Lea: Military Genius and Prophet," Historical Society of Southern California, *Quarterly,* 24:5–13 (1942).

[Lea, Homer] Newmark, Marco R. "Historical Profiles, XVI: Homer Lea," Historical Society of Southern California, *Quarterly,* 37:177–184 (1955).

[Lea, Homer] Ng Poon Chew. "The Real Homer Lea?" *The Oriental Review* (New York), 3:171–172 (1912–1913).

Leonard, Royal. *I Flew for China.* Garden City, N.Y., 1942; 295 pp.

Marsh, James Reid. *The Charm of the Middle Kingdom.* Boston, 1922; 245 pp.

[O'Banion, Ansel E.] Glick, Carl. *Double Ten, Captain O'Banion's Story of the Chinese Revolution.* London, 1945; 281 pp.

[Ward, Frederick Townsend] Abend, Hallett E. *The God from the West; A Biography of Frederick Townsend Ward.* Garden City, N.Y., 1947; 304 pp.

[Ward, Frederick Townsend] Bigelow, Poultney. "Memories of General Ward," *State Troopers' Magazine*, 2:24–25 (1921).

[Ward, Frederick Townsend] Cahill, Holger. *A Yankee Adventurer; The Story of Ward and the Taiping Rebellion*. New York, 1930; 296 pp.

[Ward, Frederick Townsend] Powell, Edward Alexander. *Gentleman Rovers*. New York, 1913; 245 pp.

[Ward, Frederick Townsend] Rantoul, Robert S. "Frederick Townsend Ward," Essex Institute, *Historical Collections*, 44:1–64, 360–370 (1908).

2.10 CHINESE WHO WENT TO THE UNITED STATES

CHINESE IN THE UNITED STATES

Biographical collections

La Fargue, Thomas E. "Some Early Chinese Visitors to the United States," *T'ien Hsia Monthly*, 11:128–139 (1940).

Individual biographies

As a Chinaman Saw Us; Passages from His Letters to a Friend at Home. New York, 1904; 324 pp.

Burdette, Mary G., comp. *Twenty Years' Work Among the Chinese in the United States, 1884–1904*. Chicago, 1904; 108 pp.

[Cameron, Donaldina MacKenzie] Wilson, Carol Green. *Chinatown Quest; The Life Adventures of Donaldina Cameron*. Stanford, 1931; 263 pp.

Condit, Ira M. *The Chinaman as We See Him, and Fifty Years of Work for Him*. Chicago, [1900]; 233 pp.

Holt, Hamilton, ed. "The Life Story of a Chinaman," *The Life Stories of Undistinguished Americans as Told by Themselves*. New York, 1906; 299 pp.

Lee, Yan Phou. *When I Was a Boy in China.* Boston, [1887]; 111 pp.

Park, No-yong. *Chinaman's Chance; An Autobiography.* Boston, 1940; 182 pp.

Huie Kin [Hsü Chin]. *Reminiscences.* Peiping, 1932; 115 pp.

Lowe, Pardee. *Father and Glorious Descendant.* Boston, 1943; 322 pp.

Wu Tingfang. *America, Through the Spectacles of an Oriental Diplomat.* New York, [1914]; 267 pp.

"AMERICA-RETURNED" CHINESE
Biographical collections

Boorman, Howard L., ed. *Men and Politics in Modern China: Preliminary 50 Biographies* (Includes articles on Hsü Chih-mo, Liu T'ing-fang, Shih Mei-yü, Wen I-to, and Yü Jih-chang.) New York, 1960; 173 pp.

Green, Katharine R. Some Christian Leaders of Present-day China. 1949; 122 pp., typewritten. MRL

La Fargue, Thomas E. *China's First Hundred.* Pullman, Wash., 1942; 176 pp.

Individual biographies

[Chao, Yuenren. Letters. Peking, 1921]; 19 pp.

[Chao, Yuenren] *Second Green Letter.* [Cambridge, Mass., 1923]; 40 pp.

[Chao, Yuenren] Grootaers, Willem. "Chao Yüan-jen, China's Leading Dialectologist," *Orbis*, 3:328–355 (1954).

Chao, Buwei Yang. *Autobiography of a Chinese Woman,* trans. Yuenren Chao. New York, 1947; 327 pp.

[Ch'en Li-fu] Didsbury, Howard F., Jr. "Chen Li-fu: A Critical Study," *Iqbal*, 5:48–70 (1957).

Chiang, Mayling Soong. *Sian: A Coup d'Etat* [and] *A*

Fortnight in Sian: Extracts from a Diary by Chiang Kai-shek. Shanghai, 1937; 119 pp.

[Chiang, Mayling Soong] Nicolay, Helen. *China's First Lady.* New York, 1944; 224 pp.

Chiang, Monlin. *Tides from the West. A Chinese Autobiography.* New Haven, 1947; 282 pp.

[Chiang, Monlin] Borowitz, Albert. "Chiang Monlin: Theory and Practice of Chinese Education, 1917–1930," *Papers on China,* 8:107–135 (1954).

[Franking, Mae M.] M. T. F. *My Chinese Marriage.* New York, 1921; 169 pp.

[Hu Shih] Grieder, Jerome B. "Hu Shih and Liberalism: A Chapter in the Intellectual Modernization of China, 1917–1930," Ph.D. thesis, Harvard University, 1963; 461 pp.

[Hu Shih] Saunders, Kenneth James. *Whither Asia? A Study of Three Leaders.* New York, 1933; 221 pp.

Koo, Hui-lan Oei, and Mary Van Rensselaer Thayer. *Hui-lan Koo. An Autobiography.* New York, 1943; 421 pp.

[K'ung Hsiang-hsi] Yu Liang. *Kung Hsiang-hsi: The Biography of a Former Premier of Nationalist China.* n.p., [1957]; 248 pp.

Liang, Thomas Pao-Ho. "Thirty-five Years and Ten Thousand Miles Ago," *Phillips Exeter Bulletin,* 53.5:6–12 (1957).

[Liu Chan-en] Liu, Frances W. *The Death of My Husband, Dr. Herman C. E. Liu.* Hongkong, 1939; 45 pp.

[Mei Yi-ch'i] "A Seventy-year Chronology of Dr. Y. C. Mei's Life and Work with Special Reference to His Association with Tsing Hua University," *Tsing Hua Journal of Chinese Studies,* New Series 2.1: special section (1960).

[Shih Chao-chi] *Sao-ke Alfred Sze: Reminiscences of His Early Years.* Washington, 1962; 77 pp.

[Soong family] Hahn, Emily. *The Soong Sisters.* New York, 1941; 349 pp.

[Soong family] Spencer, Cornelia. *Three Sisters; the Story of the Soong Family of China.* New York, 1939; 279 pp.

[T'ao Hsing-chih] Chu, Don-Chean. "T'ao Hsing-chih and Chinese Education." Ed.D. thesis, Teachers College, Columbia University, 1953; 254 pp.

[T'ao Hsing-chih] Kuhn, Philip A. "T'ao Hsing-chih, 1891–1946, An Educational Reformer," *Papers on China*, 13:163–195 (1959).

Tong, Hollington K. *China and the World Press.* Nanking, 1948; 282 pp.

Tong, Hollington K. *Dateline: China; the Beginnings of China's Press Relations with the World.* New York, 1950; 269 pp.

[Wen I-to] Hsü, Kai-yü. "The Life and Poetry of Wen I-to," *Harvard Journal of Asiatic Studies*, 21:134–179 (1958).

Wu Ching-hsiung (John C. H. Wu). *Beyond East and West.* New York, 1951; 364 pp.

[Wu Hsien] Wu, Daisy Yen. *Hsien Wu, 1893–1959; in Loving Memory.* Boston, 1959; 75 pp.

[Yen, Yang-ch'u] Buck, Pearl. *Tell the People: Talks with James Yen about the Mass Education Movement.* New York, 1945; 84 pp.

[Yung Shang Him] "Autobiography of Yung Shang Him," in Yung Shang Him, *The Chinese Educational Mission and Its Influence.* Shanghai, 1939; 47 pp.

Yung Wing. *My Life in China and America.* New York, 1909; 286 pp.

3. NEWSPAPERS AND PERIODICALS

3.1   Published in the United States
    Newspapers and magazines
    Mission magazines
      Denominational
      Nondenominational or interdenominational
    American-Chinese press: English-language editions
    Scholarly journals
3.2   Published in China (including Hongkong)
    Newspapers and magazines
      Canton
      Chungking
      Hankow
      Nanking
      Peking (Peiping)
      Shanghai
      Tientsin
      Tsingtao
      Hongkong
    Mission magazines
    Yearbooks
    Scholarly journals
      General; humanities and social sciences
      Science and technology

Under 3.1 are listed only newspapers and periodicals published in the United States which are particularly concerned with China or with the Chinese in the United States. Also included are selected mission magazines published at home, which often printed articles or letters written by China missionaries.

Section 3.2 presents Western-language newspapers and periodicals published in the China area. Many were owned by the British or other Europeans or by the Chinese, but they are valuable sources on American activities and on American influence in China. Note especially the large number of Chinese scientific journals published in English.

To locate copies of periodicals, consult: Winifred Gregory, comp., *Union List of Serials in Libraries of the United States and Canada*, 2d ed., New York, 1943; *Supplements*, 1945 and 1953; and James D. Stewart, *et al.*, eds., *British Union-Catalogue of Periodicals*, 4 vols., London, 1955–1958; *Sup-*

plement, 1962. A guide to Western-language newspapers published in China and Hongkong before 1911, including a detailed checklist of the holdings of forty libraries in the United States, Britain, France, Germany, Japan, and Hongkong, is being prepared by Frank H. H. King and Prescott Clarke. The best depository for missionary magazines is the Missionary Research Library, New York.

For all entries in this chapter, the first date given under each title is the date of first publication. The termination date for the newspaper or periodical is given only when it is definitely known. Within each section, entries are listed chronologically according to the date of first publication. The only exception is that of mission magazines published in the United States, which are arranged alphabetically according to denomination.

3.1 PUBLISHED IN THE UNITED STATES
NEWSPAPERS AND MAGAZINES

Journal of the American Asiatic Association (New York), 1898–1917; succeeded by *Asia*, 1917–1942; succeeded by *Asia and the Americas*, 1942–1946.

Far East: A Voice of the Orient (New York), 1904–   .

Chinese Students' Monthly (Baltimore, etc.), 1905–1930.

Chinese Students' Alliance of the Eastern United States, *Chinese Students' Bulletin* (New York), 1906–   .

Far East (Detroit), 1907–1909.

Chinese Defender (San Francisco), 1910–1911.

New York Chinese Students' Club, *Chinese Annual* (New York), 1911.

Far Eastern Fortnightly (New York), 1913–1921.

Chinese Students' Christian Association in North America, *Christian China*, also entitled *Chinese Students' Christian Monthly* (New York), 1914–1922; succeeded by *C.S.C.A. Fellowship Notes*, 1922–1925; succeeded by *Chinese Christian Student*, 1925–1947.

Far Eastern Republic: A Monthly Magazine Devoted to the Republic of China (San Francisco), 1919–1920.

China Trade Bureau, New York, *China Review*, 1921–1924.

Chinese Students' Alliance in the United States, *China Advocate* (Chicago; Washington), 1921– .

Office of the Trade Commissioner of South China, New York, *China Trade,* 1921– .

China Society of America, New York, *China,* 1924– .

American Committee for Fair Play in China, *Bulletin* (San Francisco), 1925– .

United States Department of Commerce, Foreign Commerce Service, *China Monthly Trade Report,* 1929– . *China Review,* 1932– .

Institute of Pacific Relations, American Council, *Far Eastern Survey* (New York), 1932–1961; succeeded by *Asian Survey* (Berkeley), 1961– .

China Today: A Monthly Magazine of Information and Opinion on the Far East (New York), 1934–1942.

China Cultural Society of America, San Francisco, *Chinese Digest,* 1935–1940.

Chinese Student (Chicago; New York), 1935–1938.

China Institute in America, New York, *China Institute Bulletin,* 1936–1947; succeeded by *America and China,* 1948–1949.

Amerasia: A Review of America and the Far East (New York), 1937–1947.

Chinese Council for Economic Research, *Bulletin* (Washington), 1937– .

Chinese Mercury: Quarterly Journal for World's English-speaking Public, with Press Comments (Columbia, Mo.), 1937–1939.

Chinese Student: The Far Eastern Magazine (New York), 1937– .

China Aid Council, etc., *Newsletter* (New York), 1938– .

Far Eastern Affairs and the American Spokesman Monthly (San Francisco), 1938–1940.

China Monthly (New York), 1939–1950.

Far Eastern News (New York), 1939–   .

American Committee in Aid of Chinese Industrial Co-operatives, New York, *INDUSCO Bulletin,* 1941–1952.

Chinese Press (San Francisco), 1941–1943.

Chinese Students' Association of the South, *China Call* (Rolla, Mo.), 1941–   .

Trans-Pacific News Service, New York, etc., *Contemporary China: A Reference Digest,* 1941–1946.

Committee on Wartime Planning for Chinese Students in the United States, *National Reconstruction* (New York), 1942–1947.

United China Relief, Inc., *News of China* (New York), 1942–1949.

China's Children Fund, *China News* (Richmond, Va.), 1943–   .

People's Foreign Relations Association of China, *Chinese Mind* (New York), 1943.

China-America Council of Commerce and Industry, *China Trade News* (New York), 1944–1947.

Chinese Agricultural Newsletter (Washington), 1944–1946.

China Industrial Critic (New York), 1945–   .

Chinese Public Opinion (Washington), 1945–1946.

Committee for a Democratic Far Eastern Policy, *Far East Spotlight* (New York), 1945–1950.

East Wind (Cleveland), 1945–1947.

Chinese News Service, New York, *China Magazine,* 1946–1949.

Far East Trader (San Francisco), 1946–   .

Asia Calling (Santa Monica, Calif.), 1947–   .

Institute of Pacific Relations, *Far East Digest* (New York), 1947–   .

Chinese News Service, *China Information Bulletin* (New York), 1948–1949.

Far Eastern Newsletter (Washington), 1948–   .

MISSION MAGAZINES

The following list does not include bulletins and annual reports issued by missionary organizations.

Denominational

Advent Christian Church, American Advent Mission Society, *Prophetic and Mission Record* (Boston), 1896–1920; succeeded by *Advent Christian Missions,* 1920–   .

(Baptist) American Baptist Convention, American Baptist Foreign Mission Society, *Massachusetts Baptist Missionary Magazine* (Boston), 1803–1816; succeeded by *Baptist Missionary Magazine,* 1817–1909; succeeded by *Missions* (Boston and New York), 1910-   .

(Baptist) American Baptist Convention, American Baptist Foreign Mission Society, *Overseas* (New York), 1929–1932; succeeded by *All Kindreds and Tongues,* 1932–   .

(Baptist) Gospel Baptist Mission, *Our Missionary Helper* (Decatur, Ga.), 1893–1902.

(Baptist) Southern Baptist Convention, Foreign Mission Board, *Foreign Mission Journal* (Richmond, Va.), 1851–1916 (title varies); succeeded by *Home and Foreign Fields* (Nashville), 1916–1937.

(Baptist) Southern Baptist Convention, Foreign Mission Board, *Commission: or, Southern Baptist Missionary Magazine* (Richmond, Va.), 1856–1861.

(Baptist) Southern Baptist Convention, Women's Missionary Union, *Our Mission Fields* (Birmingham, Ala., and Baltimore), 1906–1914; succeeded by *Royal Service,* 1914– .

(Baptist) Southern Baptist Convention, Women's Missionary Union, *World Comrades* (Birmingham, Ala.), 1922– .

Church of the Brethren, General Mission Board, *Missionary Visitor* (Elgin, Ill.), 1894–1930; merged into *Gospel Messenger* (Elgin, Ill.), 1883– .

Church of God, Missionary Board, *Gospel Trumpet* (Moundsville, W. Va., and Anderson, Ind.), 1880– .

(Congregational) American Board of Commissioners for Foreign Missions, *Panoplist* (Boston), 1805–1808; succeeded by *Panoplist and Missionary Magazine,* 1808–1817; succeeded by *Panoplist and Missionary Herald,* 1818–1820; succeeded by *Missionary Herald,* 1821–1951; succeeded by *Advance,* 1951– .

(Congregational) American Board of Commissioners for Foreign Missions, *Missionary Papers* (Boston), 1824–1838.

(Congregational) American Board of Commissioners for Foreign Missions, *Dayspring* (Boston), 1842–1849.

(Congregational) American Board of Commissioners for Foreign Missions, *Envelope Series* (Boston), 1898– .

(Congregational) American Board of Commissioners for Foreign Missions, *American Board Bulletin* (Boston), 1909– .

(Congregational) American Board of Commissioners for Foreign Missions, Women's Board of Missions, *Life and Light for Heathen Women* (Boston), 1869–1922; merged into *Missionary Herald.*

(Congregational) Women's Board of Missions of the Interior, *Mission Studies* (Chicago), 1883–1922; merged into *Missionary Herald.*

Disciples of Christ (Foreign Christian Missionary Society, 1876–1919, and United Christian Missionary Society, 1919–   ), *Missionary Tidings* (Indianapolis), 1883–1918; succeeded by *World Call* (St. Louis), 1919–   .

Disciples of Christ (Foreign Christian Missionary Society, 1876–1919, and United Christian Missionary Society, 1919–   ), *Missionary Intelligencer* (Cincinnati), 1887–1918; succeeded by *World Call* (St. Louis), 1919–   .

(Episcopalian) Protestant Episcopal Church, Domestic and Foreign Missionary Society, *Missionary Paper* (Philadelphia), 1828–1830; succeeded by *Periodical Paper,* 1831–1832; succeeded by *Missionary Record,* 1833–1835; succeeded by *Spirit of Missions* (New York and Burlington, N.J.), 1836–1939; succeeded by *Forth* (New York), 1940–   .

(Episcopalian) Protestant Episcopal Church, Board of Missions, Foreign Committee, *Foreign Missionary* (New York), 1863–1877.

Evangelical Church, Missionary Society, *Evangelical Missionary World* (Harrisburg, Pa.), 1923–   .

Evangelical Mission Covenant Church of America, Board of Missions, *Arsberättelse* (Chicago), 1885–   .

(Friends) Society of Friends, American Friends Service Committee, *Bulletin on Work in China* (Philadelphia), 1942–1947.

Hepzibah Faith Missionary Association, *John Three Sixteen* (Tabor, Ia., etc.), 1891–   .

Hepzibah Faith Missionary Association, *Good Tidings Sent of God* (Tabor, Ia.), 1914–   .

(Lutheran) Augustana Evangelical Lutheran Church, Board of Foreign Missions, *Missionsbote* (Philadelphia and Reading, Pa.), 1878–1918.

(Lutheran) Augustana Evangelical Lutheran Church, Board of Foreign Missions, *Augustana Foreign Missionary* (Rock Island, Ill.), 1903– . Title varies.

(Lutheran) Augustana Evangelical Lutheran Church, Board of Foreign Missions, *Missionstidning* (Rock Island, Ill.), 1906– .

(Lutheran) Church of the Lutheran Brethren in America, Board of Missions, *Broderbaandet* (Faribault, Minn.), 1899– .

(Lutheran) United Lutheran Church in America, *Lutheran Missionary Journal* (*Philadelphia*), 1878–1908; merged into *Lutheran Church Work*, 1908–1912, later *Lutheran*, 1919– .

(Lutheran) United Lutheran Church in America, *Foreign Missionary* (Philadelphia and Baltimore), 1880– .

(Lutheran) United Lutheran Church in America, *Lutheran Woman's Work* (Philadelphia), 1908– .

Lutheran Church (Missouri Synod), *Lutheran Witness* (St. Louis), 1882– .

Lutheran Church (Missouri Synod), *Mission Call* (Hales Corners, Wis.), 1929– .

Methodist Episcopal Church, *Missionary Advocate* (New York), 1845–1876.

Methodist Episcopal Church, *World Outlook* (New York), 1915–1920.

Methodist Episcopal Church, *Missionary Tidings for the Methodist Episcopal Church* (New York), 1879–1880.

Methodist Episcopal Church, *World-Wide Missions* (New York and Chicago), 1888–1912.

Methodist Episcopal Church, South, Board of Foreign

Missions, *Missionary Reporter,* also entitled *Methodist Review of Missions* (Nashville) 1879–1897; succeeded by *Review of Missions,* 1897–1903.

Methodist Episcopal Church, South, Board of Foreign Missions, *World for Christ* (Nashville), 1895–1899.

Methodist Episcopal Church, South, Board of Foreign Missions, *Missionary Voice* (Nashville), 1911–1932; succeeded by *World Outlook* (Nashville and New York), 1911– .

Methodist Episcopal Church, Woman's Foreign Missionary Society, *Heathen Woman's Friend* (Boston), 1869–1896; succeeded by *Woman's Missionary Friend,* 1896–1940; succeeded by *Methodist Woman* (Cincinnati), 1940– .

Methodist Protestant Church, Board of Missions, *Woman's Missionary Record* (Greensboro, N.C., and Baltimore), 1885–1924; succeeded by *Missionary Record,* 1924–1940; merged into *Methodist Woman* (Cincinnati), 1940– .

Methodist Protestant Church, Board of Missions, *Missionary Bulletin of the Methodist Protestant Church* (Lynchburg, Va.), 1890– .

Peniel Missionary Society, *Peniel Herald* (Los Angeles), 1894– .

Presbyterian Church in the U.S.A., Board of Foreign Missions, *Foreign Missionary Chronicle* (Pittsburgh and New York), 1833–1841; succeeded by *Missionary Chronicle,* 1842–1849; merged into *Home and Foreign Record of the Presbyterian Church in the United States* (Philadelphia), 1850–1867; succeeded by *Presbyterian Monthly Record,* 1868–1887; merged into *Church at Home and Abroad,* 1887–1898; merged into *Assembly Herald* (Philadelphia), 1894–1918.

Presbyterian Church in the U.S.A., Board of Foreign

Missions, *Foreign Missionary* (New York), 1842–1886; succeeded by *Church at Home and Abroad* (Philadelphia), 1887–1898; merged into *Assembly Herald* (Philadelphia), 1894–1918.

Presbyterian Church in the U.S.A., Board of Foreign Missions, *Five Continents* (New York), 1926– .

Presbyterian Church in the U.S.A., Woman's Foreign Missionary Societies, *Our Mission Field* (New York), 1871–1885; succeeded by *Woman's Work* 1886–1924 (title varies); merged into *Women and Missions* (New York), 1924– .

Presbyterian Church in the U.S.A., Woman's Home and Foreign Missionary Organizations, *Over Sea and Land* (Philadelphia), 1876–1921 (title varies); succeeded by *Missionary Mail,* 1922– .

Presbyterian Church in the U.S.A., Woman's Presbyterian Board of Foreign Missions of the Northwest, *Missionary Annals* (Chicago), 1887–1890.

Presbyterian Church in the United States, Board of World Missions, *Missionary Reporter and Education Register* (Philadelphia), 1829–1832.

Presbyterian Church in the United States, Board of World Missions, *Missionary* (Richmond, Baltimore, and Nashville), 1868–1911; succeeded by *Missionary Survey* (Richmond), 1911–1924; succeeded by *Presbyterian Survey,* 1924– .

(Presbyterian) Cumberland Presbyterian Church, Board of Missions, *Missionary Record* (St. Louis), 1875–1908.

(Presbyterian) Cumberland Presbyterian Church, Woman's Board of Missions, *Jubilee Journal* (Nashville), 1930–1931; succeeded by *Missionary Messenger,* 1931– .

(Presbyterian) First Chinese Presbyterian Church, *Chinese Christian Monitor* (New York), 1926–1927.

Reformed Church in America, *Sower and Mission Monthly* (New York), 1855–1888; succeeded by *Mission Field*, 1887–1922; merged into *Christian Intelligencer* (New York), 1829–1934.

Reformed Church in America, *Mission Gleaner* (New York), 1883–1917; merged into *Mission Field* (New York), 1887–1922.

Reformed Church in the United States, Board of Commissioners for Foreign Missions, *Reformed Missionary Herald* (Philadelphia and Lancaster, Pa.), 1880–1890; merged into *Missionary Guardian* (Philadelphia), 1891–1896; succeeded by *Reformed Church Tidings* (Bethlehem, Pa.), 1896–1900.

Reformed Church in the United States, Board of Commissioners for Foreign Missions, *Outlook of Missions* (Philadelphia), 1909– .

Reformed Presbyterian Church in North America, *Missionary Advocate* (Philadelphia), 1838–1844. Title varies.

Reformed Presbyterian Church in North America, *Olive Trees* (New York), 1887–1928; succeeded by *Covenanter Witness* (Ridgefield, N.J.), 1928– .

(Roman Catholic) Chinese Mission Society of St. Columban, *Far East, A Magazine Devoted to the Conversion of China* (Omaha, Neb.), 1876– .

(Roman Catholic) Chinese Mission Society of St. Columban, *Far East, The Magazine of the Chinese Mission Society* (St. Columbans, Neb.), 1917– .

(Roman) Catholic Foreign Mission Society of America, *Maryknoll, The Field Afar* (Maryknoll, N.Y.), 1907– .

(Roman) Catholic Foreign Mission Society of America, *Maryknoll Mission Letters, China* (New York), 1923 and

1927; succeeded by *Maryknoll Mission Letters,* 1942– .

(Roman) Catholic Foreign Mission Society of America, *Chinese-American Bulletin* (Maryknoll, N.Y.), 1942– .

(Roman Catholic) Society for the Propagation of the Faith, *Catholic Missions* (New York), 1907– .

Seventh Day Adventist Denomination, General Conference, *Advent Review and Sabbath Herald* (Washington, etc.), 1850– .

Seventh Day Adventist Denomination, General Conference, *Medical Missionary* (Battle Creek, Mich.), 1886–1914.

Seventh Day Adventist Denomination, General Conference, *Missionary Magazine* (Battle Creek, Mich.), 1889–1902. Title varies.

United Brethren in Christ, Foreign Missionary Society, *Evangel* (Dayton, O.), 1882– .

United Brethren in Christ, Domestic, Frontier and Foreign Missionary Society, *Missionary Monthly* (Huntington, Ind.), 1897– .

Nondenominational or interdenominational

American Bible Society, *Bible Society Record* (New York), 1843– .

American Bible Society, *Worldwide Biblework* (New York), 1901–1905; succeeded by *Bible in Every Land,* 1906–1911.

American Medical Missionary Society, *Medical Missionary Journal* (Chicago), 1887–1888.

Associated Boards for Christian Colleges in China, *China Colleges* (New York), 1934–1952; succeeded by *New Horizons for the China Colleges* (title varies), 1953–1955; succeeded by *New Horizons,* 1956– .

China Inland Mission, *China's Millions* (London), 1875– . American edition (Philadelphia and Toronto), 1893– .

China Inland Mission, *Land of Sinim* (London, Philadelphia, etc.), 1904–1905; succeeded by *China and the Gospel,* 1906–1937.

China Mission Advocate (Louisville), 1839. Founded by the supporters of Issacher J. Roberts.

Chinese Advocate: Organ of the Chinese Sunday Schools (New York), 1890– .

Chinese Mission Society, Far East: A Magazine Devoted to the Conversion of China (Omaha, Neb., etc.), 1876– .

Christian and Missionary Alliance, *Christian Alliance and Foreign Missionary Weekly* (Harrisburg, Pa., etc.), 1887–1896; succeeded by *Christian and Missionary Alliance,* 1897–1911; succeeded by *Alliance Weekly,* 1912– .

International Missionary Council, *International Review of Missions* (Edinburgh), 1912– .

International Union Mission, *The Messenger* (New York), 1921– .

Medical Missionary Record, 1886–1894; succeeded by *Double Cross and Medical Missionary Record* (New York), 1886–1900.

Missionary Eclectic: A Repository of Select Missionary Works, American and Foreign (Boston), 1843.

Missionary Review (Princeton), 1878–1887; succeeded by *Missionary Review of the World* (New York and London), 1888–1939.

National Council of the Churches of Christ in the U.S.A., Division of Foreign Missions, Far Eastern Joint Office, *China Bulletin* (New York), 1947– .

Scandinavian Alliance Mission of North America, *Mission-*

ary Broadcaster of the Scandinavian Alliance Mission (Chicago), 1925–   .

Woman's Union Missionary Society of America, *Missionary Link* (New York), 1861–   .

Yale-in-China, *Yali Quarterly* (New Haven), 1916–   .

YMCA of North America, International Committee, *Watchman* (Chicago), 1874–1889; succeeded by *Young Men's Era,* 1890–1896; succeeded by *Men, a Young Man's Paper,* 1896–1899; succeeded by *Association Men* (New York), 1899–1930; succeeded by *Young Men,* 1931–1933.

YMCA of North America, International Committee, *Foreign Mail* (New York), 1894–1919.

Young Women's Christian Association of the U.S.A., Foreign Division of the National Board, *Association Monthly* (New York), 1907–1922; succeeded by *Woman's Press,* 1923–   .

AMERICAN-CHINESE PRESS, ENGLISH-LANGUAGE EDITIONS

The Oriental, or Tung-Ngai San-Luk (San Francisco), 1855–   .

American and Chinese Commercial News (San Francisco), 1883–   .

Chinese of Hawaii (Honolulu), 1929–   .

SCHOLARLY JOURNALS

American Oriental Society, *Journal* (New Haven, etc.), 1843–   .

Artibus Asiae (Ascona, Switzerland; New York; etc.), 1925–   .

Institute of Pacific Relations, *Problems of the Pacific,* proceedings of conferences (Chicago, etc.), 1925–1940.

Pacific Data, from the Institute of Pacific Relations (Honolulu), 1927–1928; succeeded by *Pacific Affairs* (Honolulu; New York; Vancouver), 1928–   .

Eastern Art (Philadelphia), 1928–1931.

Pacific Historical Review (Glendale, Calif., etc.), 1932–   .

Harvard Journal of Asiatic Studies (Cambridge, Mass.), 1936–   .

American Council of Learned Societies Devoted to Humanistic Studies, Committee on Chinese and Japanese Studies, *Notes on Far Eastern Studies in America* (Washington), 1937–1943.

Claremont Oriental Studies (Claremont, Calif.), 1939–   .

Far Eastern Quarterly (Ithaca, N.Y., etc.), 1941–1956; succeeded by *Journal of Asian Studies* (Ann Arbor, etc.), 1956–   .

Far Eastern Science Bulletin (Washington), 1941–1944.

Chinese Institute of Engineers, American Section, *C.I.E. Journal* (New York), 1943–1944.

Archives of the Chinese Art Society of America (New, York), 1945–   .

Papers on China (Cambridge, Mass.), 1947–   .

Phi Theta Annual (Berkeley), 1947–   .

Association of American Geographers, Committee on Asian Studies, *Bulletin* (Hamilton, N.Y.), 1948–   .

Far Eastern Ceramic Bulletin (Cambridge, Mass.), 1948–   .

3.2 PUBLISHED IN CHINA (INCLUDING HONGKONG)
NEWSPAPERS AND MAGAZINES

Canton

Canton Register (Canton and Macao), 1827–1843.

Canton Miscellany, 1831–   .

Chinese Courier and Canton Gazette, 1831–1833.

Canton General Price Current, 1834–   .

Canton Press and Price Current (Canton and Macao), 1835–1844.

Friend of China, 1842, 1860–1861.

Canton Press, 1874.

Canton Times, 1918–   .

Political Review, 1927.

South China Monthly Review, 1928–1929.

China Truth, 1929–1933; succeeded by *Canton Truth,* 1933–   .

Canton, 1939–   .

Chungking

West China Messenger, 1902–1910.

China at War, 1938–1945; succeeded by *China Magazine* (New York), 1946–1949.

China Forum (Hankow and Chungking), 1938–1940.

China Fortnightly, 1939–1941.

China Science Service, 1944–1946.

Hankow

Hankow Herald, 1923–   .

Pan-Pacific Monthly, 1927–1930. (From June 1927 to March 1928, the title was *Pan-Pacific Worker;* from April 1928 to March 1929, the title was *Far-Eastern Monthly.*)

People's Tribune, 1927.

China at War (Hankow, etc.), 1938–   .

China Forum (Hankow and Chungking), 1938–   .

Nanking

Chinese Affairs, 1928–1934.

Far Eastern Information Bureau, *Bulletin,* 1929–1930.

Council of International Affairs, *Information Bulletin*, 1936–1937.
Voice of New China, 1938–1941.

Peking (Peiping)

China Times, 1901.
Chinese Public Opinion, 1908–1909; succeeded by *Peking Daily News*, 1909–   .
Peking Post, 1910.
Bulletin Catholique de Pékin, 1913–   .
Politique de Pékin, 1914–   .
Peking Leader, 1917–   .
North China Standard, 1919–   .
Le Chine, 1921–1925.
Chinese Government, Bureau of Economic Information, etc., *Chinese Economic Monthly*, 1923–1926; succeeded by *Chinese Economic Journal and Bulletin*, 1927–1937.
Week in China, 1924–1932 (published by the *Peking Leader*).
China Outlook, 1927–1928; succeeded by *China Tomorrow*, 1928–1930.
China (Peiping and Shanghai), 1928.
Yenching University Journalism Club, *New China*, 1930–1931.
China in Brief, 1931.
Peking Magazine, 1931.
Peking News and Views of China, 1931–   .
People's Tribune (Peiping, etc.), 1931–1941.
China Weekly Chronicle. Weekly edition of the *Peiping Chronicle*, 1932–1937.
Peiping Chronicle, 1932–   .
Caravan: Magazine of the Far East, 1936–1939.

Shanghai

Chinese Miscellany, 1849–1850.

North-China Herald, 1850–1867; then *North-China Herald and Market Report,* 1867–1870; then *North-China Herald and Supreme Court and Consular Gazette,* 1870–   .

Daily Shipping and Commercial News, 1862–1864.

Friend of China, 1863–1869.

North-China Daily News, 1864–   .

Shanghai Commercial Record, 1864–1866.

Punch, 1867.

Shanghai Newsletter for California and the Atlantic States, 1867–1873.

Supreme Court and Consular Gazette, 1867–1870.

Shanghai Evening Courier, 1868–1875.

The Cycle: A Political and Literary Review, 1870–1871.

Far East (Yokohama and Shanghai), 1870–1878.

Puck or the Shanghai Charivari, 1870–1872.

Shanghai Budget and Weekly Courier, 1871–1873.

Shanghai News-Letter, 1871–1873.

Peking Gazette, translation, 1872–   .

Evening Gazette, 1873–1875.

Celestial Empire, 1874–   .

Shanghai Budget and Weekly News-Letter, 1874–1875.

Shanghai Courier and China Gazette, 1875–1890.

Chinese Scientific and Industrial Magazine, 1876–1892.

Far East, 1876–   .

Shanghai Mercury, 1879–   .

Der Ostasiatische Lloyd, 1887–   .

Mesny's Chinese Miscellany: A Textbook of Notes on China and the Chinese, 1895–   .

The Rattle, 1896–   .

Central China Record, 1898–   .

l'Echo de Chine, 1898–   . Weekly edition, 1901–   .

American Association of China, *Journal,* 1899–   .

East of Asia Magazine, 1902–1906.

Ferne Osten, 1902–1905.

Far Eastern Review (Shanghai and Manila), 1904–1941.

Eastern Sketch, 1905–1909.

Far East, 1905–1906.

Handels nachrichten, 1907–   .

Saturday Evening Review, 1907; succeeded by *Saturday Review,* 1908–1912; succeeded by *National Review,* 1912–1916.

Shipping Review and Shipping and Engineering, 1909–   .

Capital and Commerce, 1911–   .

China Press, 1911–   .

Republican Advocate of China, 1911.

China Republican, 1913.

China Monthly Review, 1917–   .

Millard's Review of the Far East, 1917–1921; succeeded by *Weekly Review of the Far East,* 1921–1923; succeeded by *China Weekly Review,* 1923–   .

China and Far East Finance and Commerce, 1918–1925; succeeded by *Finance and Commerce,* 1925–   .

China Observer, 1918–   .

Shanghai Gazette, 1918–   .

New China Review, 1919–1922.

Oriental Motor, 1919–1924.

Finance and Commerce, 1920–1941. Title varies.

Chinese Government Bureau of Foreign Trade, etc., *Chinese Economic Bulletin* (Shanghai), 1921–1935; merged in 1936 with *Chinese Economic Journal* (Peiping), 1927–1935, and continued as *Chinese Economic Journal and Bulletin* (Shanghai), 1936–1937.

Chinese National Association for the Advancement of Education, *Bulletin,* 1922–1926.

The Orient: Occidental Life in the Far East, Published in the Interest of the U.S. Military and Naval Forces, 1924–   .

China Digest, 1925–   .

National Anti-opium Association of China, *Opium: A World Problem,* 1927–1929.

China Critic, 1928–1940.

Chinese Affairs: A Weekly Survey of Important Events Relating to China, 1928–1934.

Bank of China, *Financial and Commercial Monthly Bulletin* (Shanghai, etc.), 1930–1939.

Chinese Nation, 1930–1932.

People's Tribune: An Organ of National Revolutionary Thought and Opinion, 1931–1937.

Shanghai Spectator, 1931–   .

United China Magazine, 1931–1933.

China Forum, 1932–1934.

Chinese Republic, 1932–1936.

China Press Weekly, 1933–1937.

Far East Magazine, 1934–   .

Central Bank of China, *Bulletin,* 1935–1940.

China International Famine Relief Commission, *News Bulletin,* 1935–   .

China Outlook, 1935–1938; succeeded by *Voice of New China,* 1938–   .

Chinese Administrator, 1935.

Chinese Opinions on Current Events (translated from Chinese periodicals), 1936–   .

Far Eastern Engineer, 1937–   .

East Asia Review, 1938–   .

Shanghai International Red Cross, *News Bulletin,* 1938–1939.
China Exporter, 1939–1940.
China News and Views Digest, 1939–1941.
XX Century, 1939–1943.
Asiana, 1941.
Times Week, 1943–1945.
Chinese Industrial Cooperatives, *Gung Ho News,* 1946–1949.
China Trade Monthly, 1947–1949.
China Economist, 1948–1949.

Tientsin

Chinese Times, 1886–1891.
Peking and Tientsin Times, 1894– .
Tageblatt für Nord-china, 1904– .

Tsingtao

Die Deutsch-Asiatische Wart, 1900– .
Tsingtauer Neueste Nachrichten, 1904– .

Hongkong

Friend of China and Hongkong Gazette, 1842–1859.
Hongkong Register, 1843–1860.
China Mail, 1845– ; also *Overland China Mail,* 1848–1909.
Overland Friend of China, 1845–1859.
Overland Register and Prices Current, 1845–1861.
China Overland Trade Report, 1857–1888.
Hongkong Daily Press, 1857– . Overland edition:
  China Overland Trade Report, 1857– .

Hongkong Shipping List and Commercial Intelligencer,
    1857–1862.
Hongkong Recorder, 1859.
Hongkong Register and Daily Advertiser, 1860–   .
Overland China Chronicle, 1860–   .
Hongkong Daily Press, 1861–   .
Hongkong Mercury and Shipping Gazette, 1866.
China Punch, 1867–1868; 1872–1876.
China Magazine, 1868–1869.
Daily Advertiser, 1869–1871; succeeded by *Daily Advertiser and Shipping Gazette,* 1871–1873.
Hongkong Weekly Press and China Overland Trade Report, 1869–   .
China Review, or Notes and Queries on the Far East,
    1872–1901.
Hongkong Times, Daily Advertiser and Shipping Gazette,
    1873–1876.
Hongkong Catholic Register, 1878–1880; *Catholic Register,* 1881–1887.
Hongkong Telegraph, 1881–   .
South China Morning Post, 1903–   .
South China Weekly Post, 1903–   .
Review of the Far East, 1906–1907.
The Critic, 1932–   .
Far Eastern Mirror, 1938.
China Today, 1939–   .
Far Eastern Digest, 1939–1940.
Far East Bulletin: News and Views from China, 1940–   .
Far Eastern Economic Review, 1946–   .

MISSION MAGAZINES

This section includes a few samples of magazines published at Christian colleges and universities in China. For scholarly journals produced by these institutions, see pages 170–175.

Chinese Repository (Canton), 1832–1851.

Evangelist; and Miscellanea Sinica (Canton), 1833.

Missionary Recorder (Foochow), 1867; succeeded by *Chinese Recorder,* 1868–1872; (Shanghai), 1874– . (From 1868 to January 1912 the title was *Chinese Recorder and Missionary Journal.*)

Woman's Work in China (Shanghai), 1877–1889; succeeded by *Woman's Work in the Far East,* 1890–1921.

China Medical Missionary Journal (Shanghai), 1887–1909; succeeded by *China Medical Journal,* 1909–1931; succeeded by *Chinese Medical Journal,* 1932– .

American Board of Commissioners for Foreign Missions, *Shansi Echoes* (Shansi Province), 1889– .

Chinese Intercollegian: Official Organ of the College Young Men's Christian Association of China (Tientsin), 1896– .

West China Missionary News (Chungking and Chengtu), 1899– .

Society for the Diffusion of Christian and General Knowledge among the Chinese, *Signs of Progress in China* (Shanghai), 1900– .

China Methodist Forum (Foochow), 1902– .

Methodist Episcopal Church, *Fuhkien Witness* (Foochow), 1902– .

West China Messenger (Chungking), 1902–1910.

American Board of Commissioners for Foreign Missions, *Foochow Messenger* (Foochow), 1903–1940.

World's Chinese Student's Journal (Shanghai), 1906–1914.

YMCA, *China's Young Men* (Shanghai), 1906–1916.

China Christian Educational Association, *Educational Review* (Shanghai), 1907–1938; absorbed by the *Chinese Recorder* in 1939.

Friends' Foreign Missionary Society of Ohio Yearly Meet-
ing, *Friends Oriental News* (Nanking), 1908–   .
University of Nanking Magazine (Nanking), 1909–   .
Shanghai Baptist College, *Voice* (Shanghai), 1912–   .
China Sunday School Journal (Shanghai), 1913–1934.
China Christian Advocate (Shanghai), 1914–   .
China Bookman (Shanghai), 1918–1951.
Hinghwa (Hinghwa, Fukien), 1918–   .
American Board of Commissioners for Foreign Missions,
Fenchow (Fenchow, Shansi), 1920–   .
*China for Christ: Bulletin of the China-for-Christ Move-
ment* (Shanghai), 1920–   .
Wuchow Baptist Missioner (Wuchow, Kwangsi), 1920–   .
National Christian Council of China, *Bulletin* (Shanghai),
1922–1937.
Fukien Christian University, *Fukien Star* (Foochow),
1923–   .
China Christian Educational Association, *Bulletin* (Shang-
hai), 1924–   .
Methodist Episcopal Church, *Foochow News* (Foochow),
1924–1940.
Chinese Mission to Lepers, *Leper Quarterly* (Shanghai),
1927–1943.
Catholic Church in China, Synodal Commission, *Collec-
tanea Commissionis Synodalis* (Peiping), 1928–1947;
succeeded by *China Missionary Bulletin* (Shanghai;
Hongkong), 1948–   .
China Fundamentalist (Yencheng), 1928–   .
Irish Jesuit Fathers, *The Rock* (Hongkong), 1928–   .
Maryknoll mission, *Wuchow Bulletin* (Wuchow, Kwangsi),
1929.
St. John's Cathedral at Hongkong, *St. John's Review*
(Hongkong), 1929–   .
Catholic University of Peking, *Fu Jen News Letter* (Pei-

ping), 1931–1932; succeeded by *Fu Jen Magazine* (Peiping and Techny, Ill.), 1932–1949.

National Committee for Christian Religious Education in China, *Religious Education* (Shanghai), 1937– .

Rheinische Missions Gesellschaft, China Alliance Mission of Barmen, *Chinabote für den Amerikanischen freundeskreis der Rheinischen Mission in China* (Tungkun, via Canton), 1937–1938.

Nanking Theological Seminary Bulletin (Shanghai), 1939– .

Shanghai Hebrew Mission, *Quarterly Bulletin* (Shanghai), 1940– .

Lutheran World Federation, *China News Letter* (Shanghai, etc.), 1945– .

YEARBOOKS

China Mission Year Book (Shanghai), 1910–1925, succeeded by *China Christian Year Book,* 1926–1939.

China Year Book (London, Tientsin, etc.), 1912–1939.

Far Eastern Investor's Year-Book (Shanghai), 1925– .

Chinese Year Book (Shanghai), 1935/36–1940/41.

Chinese Government, Ministry of Information, *China Handbook, 1937–1943, A Comprehensive Survey of Major Developments in China in Six Years of War,* New York, 1943, 876 pp.; *China Handbook, 1937–1945, A Comprehensive Survey of Major Developments in China in Eight Years of War,* with 1946 supplement, New York, 1947, 862 pp.

China Annual (Shanghai), 1944.

SCHOLARLY JOURNALS

General; humanities and social sciences

Asiatic Society of China, the China Branch of the Royal Asiatic Society (Hongkong), *Transactions,* 1847–1859.

Literary and Scientific Society (Shanghai), *Journal,* 1858.

North China Branch of the Royal Asiatic Society (Shanghai), *Journal,* 1858–1948. Title varies.

Peking Oriental Society, *Journal* (Peking), 1885–1898.

Chinese Social and Political Science Review (Peking), 1916–1941.

Far Eastern Political Science Review (Canton), 1919–1920.

New China Review (Shanghai), 1919–1922.

Journal of the West China Border Research Society (Chengtu), 1922–1945.

Soochow University, Law Department, etc., *China Law Review* (Shanghai), 1922– .

China Society of Sciences and Arts and Shanghai Chemical Society, *China Journal of Science and Art* (Shanghai), 1923–1941.

Institute of Social Research, *Bulletin* (Peiping), 1928– .

Nankai Institute of Economics, Nankai University, *Nankai Weekly Statistical Service,* 1928–1933; *Monthly Bulletin on Economic China,* 1934–1935; *Nankai Social and Economic Quarterly* (Tientsin), 1935– .

China Law Journal (Shanghai), 1930–1931.

Nanking University, Foreign Relations Association, *Bulletin on China's Foreign Relations* (Nanking), 1931–1935.

Nanking University, *Nanking Journal* (Nanking), 1931– .

Yenching Series on Chinese Industry and Trade (Peiping), 1932– .

Chinese Economic and Statistical Review (Shanghai), 1934–1941.

Chinese Sociological Bulletin (Peiping), 1934.

Quarterly Bulletin of Chinese Bibliography (Peiping, etc.), 1934–1948.

Catholic University of Peking, *Monumenta Serica: Journal of Oriental Studies of the Catholic University of Peking* (Peiping, etc.), 1935–   .

China Quarterly (Shanghai), 1935–1941.

T'ien Hsia Monthly (Shanghai), 1935–1941.

Institute of Railway Economics, *Quarterly Review of Chinese Railways* (Nanking), 1936–1937.

Nanking University, Department of Agricultural Economics, *Economic Facts* (Nanking), 1936–1946.

Numismatic Society of China, *Bulletin* (Shanghai), 1937–   .

Yenching Journal of Social Studies (Peiping), 1938–1949.

Catholic University of Peking, *Folklore Studies* (Peiping), 1942–   .

Philobiblon: A Review of Chinese Publications (Nanking), 1946–1948.

Science and technology

China Medical Missionary Journal (Shanghai), 1887–1909; succeeded by *China Medical Journal,* 1909–1931; succeeded by *Chinese Medical Journal,* 1932–   .

Engineering Society of China, *Proceedings* (Shanghai), 1901–1939; succeeded by *Journal,* 1939–   .

National Medical Journal of China (Shanghai, etc.), 1915–1931; merged into *Chinese Medical Journal.*

Geological Survey of China, *Bulletin* (Peking, etc.), 1919–1948; *Memoirs,* 1919–   .

Lingnan University, Freeman Meteorological Observatory, *Daily Meteorological Record* (Canton), 1919–1926.

Association of Chinese and American Engineers, *Journal* (Peking), 1920–1937.

Peking Union Medical College, Department of Pharmacology, *Collected Papers* (Peking), 1920–   .

Lingnan   Agricultural   Review   (Canton),   1921–1927; merged into *Lingnan Science Journal*.

Peking Union Medical College, Department of Physiology, *Contributions*, 1921–1938.

Peking Union Medical College, *Selected Contributions* (Peking), 1921–1926.

Shantung Christian (Cheeloo) University, School of Medicine, *Bulletin* (Tsinan), 1921–   .

China Institution of Mining and Metallurgy, *Bulletin* (Peking), 1922–1924.

Geological Society of China, *Bulletin* (Peking), 1922–1948.

Geological Survey of China, *Palaeontologia Sinica* (Peking, etc.), 1922–1948.

Lingnan Science Journal (Canton), 1922–1942.

Science Society of China, *Transactions* (Shanghai), 1922–1947.

Nanking University, College of Agriculture and Forestry, *Agriculture and Forestry Notes* (Nanking), 1923–   ; *Bulletin* (Nanking), 1924–   .

Epidemic Prevention Bureau, *Monthly Returns (by Province) of the Prevalence of Communicable Diseases in China* (Peking), 1925–   .

Science Society of China, Biological Laboratory, *Contributions* (Nanking), 1925–1929.

Peking Society of Natural History, *Bulletin*, 1926–   .

Soochow University, Biological Supply Service, *Bulletin*, 1926–   .

Chinese Journal of Physiology (Peiping), 1927–1949.

Academia Sinica, National Research Institute of Geology, *Memoirs* (Shanghai), 1928–1936.

Fukien Christian University, Natural History Society, *Proceedings* (Foochow), 1928–1930.

Academia Sinica, Metropolitan Museum of Natural History, *Contributions* (Nanking), 1929–1930.

Academia Sinica, National Research Institute of Meteorology, *Memoirs* (Nanking), 1929–1946.

National University of Peking, *Science Quarterly* (Peiping), 1929–1935; *Science Reports,* 1936–1937.

Shanghai Science Institute, *Bulletin,* 1929– ; *Journal,* 1932– .

Academia Sinica, National Research Institute of Chemistry, *Memoirs* (Shanghai), 1930–1933; *Contributions,* 1934–1937.

Academia Sinica, National Research Institute of Engineering, *Memoirs* (Shanghai), 1930– .

National Central University, *Science Reports* (Nanking), 1930–1936.

Yenching University, Department of Biology, *Bulletin,* 1930; merged into Peking Society of Natural History, *Bulletin.*

Geological Survey of China, *Soil Bulletin* (Peiping, etc.), 1931–1945.

National Academy of Peiping, Botanical Institute, *Contributions* (Peiping), 1931–1936.

National Tsing Hua University, *Science Reports* (Peiping), 1931–1948.

St. John's University, *Biological Bulletin* (Shanghai), 1931– .

Academia Sinica, National Research Institute of Psychology, *Contributions* (Peiping), 1932– .

Fisheries Experiment Station, Canton, *Contributions* (Canton), 1932– .

Shanghai Science Institute, *Journal* (Shanghai), 1932–1948.

Chinese Chemical Society, *Journal* (Peiping), 1933– .

Chinese Journal of Physics (Shanghai), 1933–1949.

National Agricultural Research Bureau, *Crop Reports* (Nanking and Chungking), 1933–1939; *Agricultura Serica,* 1934–   .

Amoy University, *Natural Science Bulletin* (Amoy), 1934–   .

Geographical Society of China, *Journal* (Nanking), 1934–1938.

Lingnan Agricultural Journal (Canton), 1934–1936.

National Academy of Peiping, Institute of Chemistry, *Contributions* (Peiping), 1934–1936.

Yenching University, College of Natural Sciences, *Science Notes* (Peiping), 1934–   .

Chinese Botanical Society, *Bulletin* (Peiping), 1935–1937.

Chinese Journal of Zoology (Nanking), 1935–1937.

Chinese Journal of Botany (Peiping), 1936–   .

Chinese Journal of Experimental Biology (Shanghai), 1936–1940.

Chinese Journal of Psychology (Peiping), 1936–1937.

Chinese Mathematical Society, *Journal* (Shanghai), 1936–1937.

University of Amoy, *Amoy Marine Biological Bulletin,* 1936–1937.

Academia Sinica, National Institute of Zoology and Botany, *Memoirs* (Nanking), 1937–   .

Fukien Christian University Science Journal (Foochow), 1938–   .

Academia Sinica, *Science Record* (Chungking, etc.), 1942–1952.

Acta Brevia Sinensia (Chungking), 1943–1944; succeeded by *Science and Technology in China* (Nanking), 1948–1949.

Amoy University, *Collected Papers in Science and Engineering* (Chanting, Fukien), 1943–1944.

Ministry of Agriculture and Forestry, *Chinese Journal of Scientific Agriculture* (Chungking), 1943–1944.

Fukien Agricultural College, Institute of Agriculture and Forestry, *Research Bulletin* (Yungan, etc.), 1945–1947.

Chinese Journal of Nutrition (Anshun, Kweichow), 1946–1947.

Academia Sinica, Institute of Botany, *Botanical Bulletin* (Shanghai), 1947–1948.

Chinese Journal of Medical History (Shanghai), 1947–1948.

Chinese Geophysical Society, *Journal* (Nanking), 1948–   .

4. REFERENCE WORKS

The reader should be familiar with the key reference works listed in the *Harvard Guide to American History*, Part II. Here attention is drawn particularly to works valuable for the study of American activities in China or American influence upon the Chinese.

4.1 BIBLIOGRAPHIES: GENERAL

BIBLIOGRAPHICAL AIDS

American Universities Field Staff, Inc. *A Selected Bibliography: Asia, Africa, Eastern Europe, Latin America.* New York, 1960; 534 pp. *Supplement*, 1961; 75 pp.

Bureau of International Exchange, *List of Chinese Government Publications*. [Shanghai], 1930; 67 pp.

Ceadel, E. B. "Far Eastern Collections in Libraries in Great Britain, France, Holland and Germany," *Asia Major*, New Series 3.2:213–222 (1952).

Conover, Helen F. *China: A Selected List of References on Contemporary Economic and Industrial Development with Special Emphasis on Postwar Reconstruction*, rev. ed. Washington, 1946; 118 pp. (1st ed. 1945).

Cordier, Henri. *Bibliotheca Sinica: Dictionnaire bibliographique des ouvrages relatifs à l'Empire chinois*, 2d ed., rev., cor., and augmented. Paris, 1904–1908; 4 vols. *Supplément et index*. Paris, 1922–1924. Author index to the *Bibliotheca Sinica*, comp. by the East Asiatic Library, Columbia University. New York, 1953; 84 pp.

Fairbank, John K. *Bibliographical Guide to Modern China; Works in Western Languages*. Cambridge, Mass., 1948; 80 pp.

Far Eastern Bibliography. Published as part of *Far Eastern Quarterly*, Ithaca, N.Y., etc., 1941–1955 (as annual issue, 1949–1955); continued by *Bibliography of Asian Studies*, annual issue of *Journal of Asian Studies*, Ann Arbor, etc., 1956– .

Gardner, Charles S. *A Union List of Selected Western Books on China in American Libraries*, 2d ed., rev. and enl. Washington, 1938; 111 pp. (1st ed. 1932; 48 pp.)

Hucker, Charles O. *China: A Critical Bibliography*. Tucson, 1962; 125 pp.

Kerner, Robert J. *Northeastern Asia: A Selected Bibliography*. Berkeley, 1939; 2 vols.

Paauw, Douglas S., and John K. Fairbank. *Bibliography of Modern China, Works in Western Languages (Re-*

vised). Section 5: Economic. Cambridge, Mass., 1951; 50 pp.

Pritchard, Earl H., ed. *Bulletin of Far Eastern Bibliography.* Washington, 1936–1940. Beginning in 1941, issued as part of the *Far Eastern Quarterly* (since 1956, the *Journal of Asian Studies*).

Probsthain, Arthur. *Encyclopaedia of Books on China.* London, 1927; 283 pp.

Rabe, Valentin H. *American-Chinese Relations, 1784–1941; Books and Pamphlets Extracted from the Shelf Lists of Widener Library.* Cambridge, Mass., 1960; 126 pp.

Revue Bibliographique de Sinologie. Paris, 1957–   .

Taylor, Louise Marion, comp. *Catalog of Books on China in the Essex Institute.* Salem, Mass., 1926; 392 pp.

Tokyo, Tōyō Bunko. *Authors Index of a Classified Catalogue of Books in European Languages in the Tōyō Bunko, 1917–1936.* Tokyo, 1951; 149 pp.

Tokyo, Tōyō Bunko. *Catalogue of the Asiatic Library of Dr. G. E. Morrison, Now a Part of the Oriental Library, Tokyo, Japan.* Tokyo, 1924; 2 vols.

Tokyo, Tōyō Bunko. *A Classified Catalogue of Books in European Languages in the Tōyō Bunko, 1917–1936.* Tokyo, 1944; 402 pp.

United States Department of State, Office of Intelligence Research, External Research Staff. *Research on China, Completed and in Progress.* Title varies. Washington, 1953–   . Annual issues.

Windemeyer, Margaret. *China and the Far East, 1889–99. Contribution toward a Bibliography.* Albany, 1901. (*New York State Library Bulletin 59. Bibliography 25,* pp. 563–679.)

Yuan, Tung-li. *China in Western Literature; A Continua-*

tion of Cordier's Bibliotheca Sinica. New Haven, 1958; 802 pp.

Yuan, Tung-li. *Economic and Social Development of Modern China: A Bibliographical Guide.* New Haven, 1956; 130, 87 pp.

GUIDES TO REFERENCE WORKS

Fairbank, John K., comp. *Ch'ing Documents, An Introductory Syllabus,* 2d ed., rev. and enl. Cambridge, Mass., 1959; 2 vols.

Garde, P. K. *Directory of Reference Works Published in Asia.* [Paris, 1956]; 139 pp.

Ting, Joseph C. "A Preliminary Bibliography of Bibliographies on Chinese Studies," *Collectanea Commissionis Synodalis,* 14.6:551–561 (1941); 14.11:1057–1077 (1941); 14.12:1193–1207 (1941); 15.1:92–114 (1942).

GUIDES TO NEWSPAPERS AND PERIODICALS

Bates, Miner Searle. *An Introduction to Oriental Journals in Western Languages, with an Annotated Bibliography of Representative Articles.* Nanking, 1933; 65 pp.

Britton, Roswell S. *The Chinese Periodical Press, 1800–1912.* Shanghai, 1933; 151 pp.

Carl Crow, Inc. *Newspaper Directory of China (including Hongkong)* . . . Shanghai, 1931– . . Note especially the 1937 issue.

Chao, Thomas Ming-heng. *The Foreign Press in China.* Shanghai, [1931]; 114 pp.

Cordier, Henri. "La Presse Européene en Chine," *Revue de l'Extreme Orient,* 1:121 (1882).

Johnsen, Julia E. *Selected Articles on China Yesterday and Today.* New York, 1928; lxxviii, 362 pp.

Leduc, Henri. "Liste des Publications Periodiques en Extreme-Oriente," *T'oung Pao,* 4.4:371–372 (1893).

Lin Yutang. *A History of the Press and Public Opinion in China.* Chicago, 1936; 179 pp.

Löwenthal, Rudolf, *et al. The Religious Periodical Press in China.* Peiping, 1940; 2 vols.

Löwenthal, Rudolf. "Western Literature on Chinese Journalism, A Bibliography," *Nankai Social and Economic Quarterly,* 9:1007–1086 (1937).

Patterson, Don D. *The Journalism of China.* Columbia, Mo., 1922; 89 pp.

Robinson, Ednah. "Chinese Journalism in California," *Out West,* 16:33–42 (1902).

Smith, William Allan and Francis Lawrence Kent. *World List of Scientific Periodicals Published in the Years 1900–1950.* 3d ed. London, 1952; 1058 pp.

Stewart, James Douglas, and M. E. Hammond and E. Saenger. *British Union-Catalogue of Periodicals; A Record of the Periodicals of the World, from the Seventeenth Century to the Present Day, in British Libraries.* London, 1955–1958; 4 vols. *Supplement,* 1962.

Teng Yen-lin. "A Preliminary List of Periodicals and Serials in Western Languages Published in China," *Quarterly Bulletin of Chinese Bibliography* (English edition), 1:184–198 (1934).

United States Library of Congress, Periodical Division. *A Check List of Foreign Newspapers in the Library of Congress.* Washington, 1929; 209 pp.

United States Library of Congress, Science Division. *Chinese Scientific and Technical Serial Publications in the Collection of the Library of Congress.* Washington, 1955; 55 pp.

Walker, Richard L. *Western Language Periodicals on China: A Selective List.* New Haven, 1949; 30 pp.

GUIDES TO THESES

Columbia University, East Asiatic Library. *Columbia University Masters' Essays and Doctoral Dissertations on Asia, 1875–1956.* New York, 1957; 96 pp.

Irick, Robert L., Ying-shih Yü and Kwang-Ching Liu. *American-Chinese Relations, 1784–1941: A Survey of Chinese-Language Materials at Harvard.* Cambridge, Mass., 1960; 296 pp. Appendix A, "American Ph.D. Theses (1909–1956)," pp. 257–274; Appendix B, "Harvard Seminar Papers (1948–1960) and Senior Honors Theses (1935–1959)," pp. 275–278.

Person, Laura. *Cumulative List of Doctoral Dissertations and Master's Theses in Foreign Missions and Related Subjects as Reported by the Missionary Research Library's Occasional Bulletin, 1950 to 1956.* New York, 1961; 46 pp.

Stucki, Curtis W. *American Doctoral Dissertations on Asia, 1933–1958.* Ithaca, N.Y., 1959; 131 pp.

University of Chicago, Far Eastern Library. *Doctoral Dissertations and Masters' Theses on Asia, 1894–1962.* Chicago, 1962; 52 pp.

Yuan, Tung-li. *A Guide to Doctoral Dissertations by Chinese Students in America, 1905–1960.* Washington, 1961; 250 pp.

4.2 BIBLIOGRAPHIES: TOPICAL
TRADE AND INVESTMENT

Albion, Robert G. *Maritime and Naval History: An Annotated Bibliography,* rev. ed. Mystic, Conn., 1955; 93 pp.

Bromberg, Erik. "A Bibliography of Theses and Dissertations Concerning the Pacific Northwest and Alaska," *Pacific Northwest Quarterly*, 40:203–252 (1949).

Bromberg, Erik. "A Further Bibliography of Theses Concerning the Pacific Northwest and Alaska," *Pacific Northwest Quarterly*, 42:147–166 (1951).

China, Inspectorate General of Customs. *Catalogue of Customs Publications*. Shanghai, 5th issue dated 1934.

Cox, Edward Godfrey. *A Reference Guide to the Literature of Travel, Including Voyages, Geographical Descriptions, Adventures, Shipwrecks and Expeditions.* Seattle, 1935–1949; 3 vols.

Kyoto University, Dept. of Economics. *Bibliography on the Industry and Mining in China in European Languages.* [Kyoto], 1940; 2 vols.

Larson, Henrietta M., ed. *Guide to Business History; Materials for the Study of American Business History and Suggestions for Their Use.* Cambridge, Mass., 1948; 1181 pp.

Snyder, James Wilbert, Jr. "A Bibliography for the Early American China Trade, 1784–1815," *Americana*, 34:297–345 (1940).

MISSIONARIES

Bibliographia missionaria. Rome, etc., 1934–   . Annual volumes.

Catalogue of Publications of Protestant Missionaries in China. [Shanghai, 1876]; 52 pp.

Chu, Clayton H. *American Missionaries in China: Books, Articles and Pamphlets Extracted from the Subject Catalogue of the Missionary Research Library.* Cambridge, Mass., 1960; 509 pp.

Clayton, George A. *A Classified Index to the Chinese*

Literature of the Protestant Churches in China. [Hankow], 1918; 260 pp. 2d ed., ed. M. Verne McNeely, 1933; 3d ed., ed. M. Verne McNeely, 1936.

Haugsted, Ejler, ed. *Katalog over Vahls Missionsbibliotek i Statsbiblioteket i Aarhus.* Copenhagen, 1942; 373 pp.

Jackson, Samuel Macauley, and George William Gilmore, comps. *Bibliography of Foreign Missions.* New York, 1891; 661 pp.

MacGillivray, Donald, comp. *Descriptive and Classified Missionary Centenary Catalogue of Current Christian Literature, 1907, Continuing That of 1901.* Shanghai, 1907; 156 pp.

Mode, Peter G. *Source Book and Bibliographical Guide for American Church History.* Menasha, Wis., 1921; 735 pp.

Murray, John Lovell. *A Selected Bibliography of Missionary Literature.* New York, 1912; 40 pp.

Yale University, Divinity School, Day Missions Library. *Catalogue of the Foreign Mission Library of the Divinity School of Yale University,* New Haven, 1895–1902; 6 vols. in one.

CHINESE WHO WENT TO THE UNITED STATES

"Chinese Authorship in America: A Bibliography of All Available Books on China Written by Chinese and Published in the United States since 1903," *Chinese Christian Student,* 10:26–27 (1934).

Claremont Colleges Library, comp. *Materials on the Pacific Area; in the Oriental Library of Claremont Colleges Library and in the Libraries of Pomona College and Scripps College, Claremont, California.* Claremont, Calif., 1939; 141 pp.

Claremont Colleges Library. *Materials on the Pacific*

Area, in Selected Libraries of the Los Angeles Region. A Second Checklist. Claremont, Calif., 1943–1944; 3 parts.

Cowan, Robert Ernest, and Boutwell Dunlap. *Bibliography of the Chinese Question in the United States.* San Francisco, 1909; 68 pp.

Uchida Naosaku. *The Overseas Chinese; A Bibliographical Essay Based on the Resources of the Hoover Institution.* Stanford, 1959; 134 pp.

United States, Library of Congress, Division of Bibliography. *Select List of References on Chinese Immigration.* Washington, 1904; 31 pp.

DIPLOMATIC RELATIONS

Bemis, Samuel Flagg, and Grace Gardner Griffin. *Guide to the Diplomatic History of the United States, 1775–1921.* Washington, 1935; 979 pp.

Foreign Affairs Bibliography; A Selected and Annotated List of Books on International Relations. New York, 1933, 1945, 1955; 3 vols.

United States, Library of Congress, Division of Bibliography. *List of References on the United States Consular Service.* Washington, 1905; 27 pp.

Ware, Edith Ellen. *The Study of International Relations in the United States: Survey for 1937.* New York, 1938; 540 pp.

WESTERN INFLUENCE IN CHINA

Academia Sinica, National Research Council. *Scientific Bibliography of China.* Nanking, 1936; 9 parts.

Chow Tse-tsung. *Research Guide to "The May Fourth Movement."* Cambridge, Mass., 1963; 297 pp.

Israel, John. *The Chinese Student Movement, 1927–1937;*

A Bibliographical Essay Based on the Resources of the Hoover Institution. Stanford, 1959; 29 pp.

Teng, Ssu-yü, and John K. Fairbank. *Research Guide for "China's Response to the West: A Documentary Survey, 1839–1923."* Cambridge, Mass., 1954; 84 pp.

United States Bureau of Foreign and Domestic Commerce. *Finding List. Bibliography of Modern Chinese Law in the Library of Congress.* [Washington, 1944]; 48 pp.

4.3 DIRECTORIES OF PERSONS

"OLD CHINA HANDS"

American University Club of Shanghai. *American University Men in China.* Shanghai, 1936; 233 pp.

Berkeley Chamber of Commerce. *Old China Hands: A Roster,* 3d ed., rev. and enl. Berkeley, 1945; 70 pp.

Directory of China; Official, Business and Residential Directory for the Principal Ports and Cities of China, 1947, 1948. Shanghai Section. Shanghai, 1947–48; 2 vols.

The Hongkong Almanack and Directory for 1846. Hongkong, 1846; 74 pp.

The Hongkong Directory, with List of Foreign Residents in China. Hongkong, 1859; 93 pp.

Men of Shanghai and North China; a Standard Biographical Reference Work. 2d ed. Shanghai, 1935; 729 pp.

Rosenstock's Directory of China and Manila . . . Manila, 1903–   .

MISSIONARIES

Boynton, Charles Luther. Alphabetical card file of Christian missionaries in China, 1807–*ca.* 1942. MRL

Boynton, Charles Luther. "Missionaries to China, 1807–1942; a Chronological List." 481 pp. typewritten. MRL

China Inland Mission. *List of Missionaries and their Stations*. Shanghai, 1910, 1914, 1917, 1920, 1922–1924; 7 vols.

Directory of Protestant Missionaries in China, Japan and Corea. Hongkong, 1881[?]– . Title varies: 1881–1884: *List of Protestant Missionaries in China, Japan and Siam;* 1886–1891: *Directory of Protestant Missionaries in China, Corea, Siam and the Straits Settlements*.

Missionary Cameralog. West China. South China. 2 booklets issued by the American Baptist Foreign Mission Society, *ca.* 1921, containing lists of names of Baptist missionaries to West and South China from the beginning to 1921.

Protestant Episcopal Church. *List of Missionaries and their Stations [of the] American Church Mission, 1911–1934*. Various dates; approximately 500 pp.

MEDICAL MISSIONARIES

Medical Missionary Association of China. *List of Members . . . with Appendix Giving Name and Location of All Other Medical Missionaries in China*. n.p., 1923; 26 pp.

Wang, Chi-min, and Wilfred Stephen Flowers. *Directory of Christian Medical Work and Prayer Cycle, 1947–1948*. Shanghai, [1948]; 42 pp.

CHINESE IN THE UNITED STATES

China Institute in America. *Directory of Chinese University Graduates and Students in America*. New York, 1943– .

Chinese Chamber of Commerce of New York. *Chinese-American Trade; Annual and Directory, English Section, 1937*. New York, 1937; 291 pp.

Chinese Publicity Bureau, Seattle. *Chinese Business Di-*

rectory and Residents, Seattle-Tacoma-Spokane and Vicinity, ed. Mor Cheolin. Seattle, 1950; 70 pp.

Chinese Students' Alliance in the Eastern States of the United States of America. *Directory*. 1911– .

Chinese Students Handbook Co. *The Handbook of Chinese Students in U.S.A.* New York, 1929– .

Directory of Chinese Students in America. New York, 1911–1952.

Dunbar, A. R. *A. R. Dunbar's International Chinese Directory*. San Francisco, 1892–1901. Title varies.

Liu, Ling. *The Chinese in North America*. Los Angeles, 1949; 308 pp.

San Francisco Chinese Directory; Including Oakland-East Bay Section, 1949. [San Francisco], 1949; 72 pp.

Sino-American Publicity Bureau, New York. *Chinese Directory of the Eastern States, 1953–54*. New York, 1954; 1 vol.

United Chinese Association of New England, Boston. *The Chinese Directory of New England*. Boston, 1931; 96 pp.

Van Norden, Warner M. *Who's Who of the Chinese in New York*. New York, 1918; 148 pp.

WHO'S WHO IN CHINA

American University Club of Shanghai. *American University Men in China*. Shanghai, 1936; 233 pp.

Asia's Who's Who, 3d ed. Hongkong, 1960; 939 pp.

Boorman, Howard L., ed. *Men and Politics in Modern China: Preliminary 50 Biographies*. New York, 1960; 173 pp.

China, Ministry of Information. *Chinese Who's Who*. Chungking, 1943; 75 pp. A reprint from the *China Handbook 1937–1943*.

Directory of Nanking Foreign Residents and Chinese

Returned Students, With Notes and Explanations in English and Chinese, June 1918. Supplement to *Nanking Union Church Bulletin.*

Foreign Trade Association of China. *Directory of Importers and Exporters in China.* Shanghai, 1948; 1 vol.

Harvard University, Committee on International and Regional Studies, "Biographies of Kuomintang Leaders," Cambridge, Mass., 1948; 1 vol.

Hummel, Arthur W., ed. *Eminent Chinese of the Ch'ing Period (1644–1912).* Washington, 1943–1944; 2 vols.

Perleberg, Max. *Who's Who in Modern China (from the Beginning of the Chinese Republic to the End of 1953).* Hongkong, 1954; 428 pp.

Tsing Hua College. *Who's Who of American Returned Students.* Peking, 1917; 215 pp.

Walker, Merle R. *Contemporary Chinese Leaders.* New York, 1922; 31 pp.

Who's Who in China. Shanghai, 1918–1919, 1920, 1926, 1928 (supplement), 1931, 1933 (supplement), 1936–1937, 1940 (supplement), and 1950.

Who's Who in the Far East. Hongkong, 1906–1909.

Wu, Eugene. *Leaders of Twentieth-Century China: An Annotated Bibliography of Selected Chinese Biographical Works in the Hoover Library.* Stanford, 1956; 106 pp.

4.4 DIRECTORIES OF INSTITUTIONS

ORGANIZATIONS IN THE UNITED STATES CONCERNED WITH CHINA

China-America Council of Commerce and Industry. *Directory of the China-America Council of Commerce and Industry; A Guide to Nearly 400 American Companies*

Interested in Developing Trade Between China and the U.S.A. New York, 1946; 359 pp.

Fairbank, Wilma. *Directory of Organizations in America Concerned with China.* Washington, 1942; 116 pp.

Morehouse, Ward, ed. *American Institutions and Organizations Interested in Asia: A Reference Directory.* New York, 1957; 510 pp. 2d ed., ed. Ward Morehouse and Edith Ehrman, 1961; 581 pp.

WESTERN FIRMS IN CHINA

Americans and American Firms in China; Directory. [Shanghai], 1946; 170 pp.

Checklist of firms which corresponded with Augustine Heard & Co. 2 folders, typewritten. HU:BL

China, Bureau of Foreign Trade. *China Importers and Exporters Directory.* Shanghai, [1936]; 700 pp.

The China Directory. Hongkong, 1860–1876.

China Hong List: General and Business Directory for Shanghai and the Principal Ports and Cities of China. Shanghai, 1932– .

COMACRIB [Commercial Credit Information Bureau] Directory of China, Combined Chinese-Foreign Commercial and Classified Directory of China and Hong Kong. Shanghai, ca. 1925– .

Credit Men's Business Directory of China (with which is amalgamated *Rosenstock's Business Directory of China*). Shanghai, 1934, 1935; 2 vols.

The Directory & Chronicle for China, Japan, Corea . . . Hongkong, 1889–1941. (Until 1902, issued under title: *The Chronicle & Directory.*)

Wright, Arnold, and H. A. Cartwright, eds. *Twentieth Century Impressions of Hongkong, Shanghai, and Other*

Treaty Ports of China: Their History, People, Commerce, Industries, and Resources. London, 1908; 848 pp.

MISSIONS

Boynton, Charles Luther, *et al. Directory of Protestant Missions in China.* Shanghai, 1916–1950.

Boynton, Charles Luther and Charles Dozier, eds. *Handbook of the Christian Movement in China under Protestant Auspices.* Shanghai, 1936; 352 pp.

China Mission Handbook. Shanghai, 1896; 335 pp.

Hutchinson, Paul. *A Guide to Important Mission Stations in Eastern China (Lying Along the Main Routes of Travel).* Shanghai, 1920; 184 pp.

Missionary Research Library. *North American Protestant Foreign Mission Agencies.* 5th ed., New York, 1962; 119 pp.

Stauffer, Milton T., *et al. The Christian Occupation of China; A General Survey of the Numerical Strength and Geographical Distribution of the Christian Forces in China, Made by the Special Committee on Survey and Occupation, China Continuation Committee, 1918–1921.* Shanghai, 1922; 468 pp.

CHRISTIAN EDUCATIONAL INSTITUTIONS

China Christian Educational Association. *Faculty Directory: Christian Colleges and Professional Schools of China, 1928–1929.* Shanghai, 1929; 37 pp.

China Christian Educational Association. *Handbook of Christian Colleges and Universities, 1926, Including Statistical Reports for . . . 1925.* Shanghai, 1926; 45 pp.

Educational Association of China. *Mission Educational Directory for China, Containing a Brief Description of*

Educational Institutions Connected with Protestant Missions; with a List of the Protestant Missionaries in the Chinese Empire. Shanghai, 1895–1910.

Educational Association of China. *Records of the 1st–6th Triennial Meeting, 1893–1909.* Shanghai, 1893–1909; 6 vols.

The Educational Directory of China . . . A Reference Book for All Interested in Western Education in China. Shanghai, 1914–1921.

Gee, Nathaniel Gist. *The Educational Directory for Schools and Colleges Connected with Protestant Missions and Also Government and Private Schools under Foreign Supervision.* 2d issue. n.p., 1905; 142, lxviii pp.

Mosher, Gouverneur Frank. *Institutions Connected with the American Church Mission in China.* New York, [1913?]; 93 pp.

Sites, Clement Moore Lacey. *Handbook of Educational Institutions of the Methodist Episcopal Church in China.* Shanghai, 1907; 53 pp.

CHINESE CULTURAL ORGANIZATIONS

Chuang Wen-ya [Chyne, W. Y.]. *Handbook of Cultural Institutions in China.* Shanghai, 1936; 282 pp.

Lin, Mousheng. *A Guide to Chinese Learned Societies and Research Institutes.* New York, 1936; 48 pp.

4.5 COLLECTIONS OF TREATIES AND AGREEMENTS

Carnegie Endowment for International Peace, Division of International Law. *Treaties and Agreements with and Concerning China, 1919–1929.* Washington, 1929; 282 pp.

Ch'en, Yin-ching, ed. *Treaties and Agreements between*

the Republic of China and Other Powers, 1929–1954
. . . Washington, 1957; 491 pp.

China, Inspectorate General of Customs. *Treaties, Conventions, etc., Between China and Foreign States.* 2d ed., Shanghai, 1917; 2 vols.

MacMurray, John V. A., ed. *Treaties and Agreements with and Concerning China, 1894–1919* . . . New York, 1921; 2 vols.

4.6   ATLASES AND PLACE-NAME DICTIONARIES

China, Directorate General of Posts. *China Postal Atlas, Showing the Postal Establishments and Postal Routes in Each Province.* Nanking, 1936; 30 plates. (A revision of the *Chung-hua yu-cheng yü-t'u, Postal Atlas of China,* issued in 1903, 1908, and 1919.)

Dingle, Edwin John, ed. *The New Atlas and Commercial Gazetteer of China* . . . Shanghai, [1917]; *ca.* 225 pp.

Herrman, Albert. *Historical and Commercial Atlas of China.* Cambridge, Mass., 1935; 112 pp.

Playfair, G. M. H. *The Cities and Towns of China, A Geographical Dictionary,* 2d ed. Shanghai, 1910; 582, lxxvi pp. (1st ed. Hongkong, 1879; 417, lviii pp.)

Rajchman, Marthe. *A New Atlas of China: Land, Air and Sea Routes.* New York, 1941; 24 pp.

Stanford, Edward. *Atlas of the Chinese Empire; Containing Separate Maps of the Eighteen Provinces of China Proper . . . and of the Four Great Dependencies . . . together with an Index to all the Names on the Maps and a List of all Protestant Mission Stations, &c.* London, [1908]; 16 pp.

INDEX